PYTHON FOR

BEGINNER TO ADVANCE

SUBIR PAUL
B Tech, M Tech, Ph.D
Professor Jadavpur UNIVERSITY KOLKATA INDIA
https://sptech.co.in/

Rajkrishna paul
B.S Engineering(USA),
Master Robotics(France)

Chandranil Paul
Bachelor Edu (CU) IT (Commerce Finance

Preface

This book is written for all levels of people , Science, Engineering, Commerce, Business and Humanities who are interested for to have career in IT and software development which is the main global job market.

The book has been a special thrust on Artificial Intelligence (AI) in Python to enable readers to solve real day to day problems.

In addition, Modeling and Simulation of scientific and engineering problems from experimental and real data are elaborately described The book will teach you how to develop python programs to predict process, properties and structure degradation.

Process optimization and cost minima profit maxima by linear programming, is the aim of the book.

The book is for beginners to advance level to the students and professionals in all spheres of education. Readers know how to build a mathematical modeling of a real problem in plant or engineering.

The prerequisite of the book is not only for those who have knowledge on programming but for also beginners who have urge to learn and develop.

It starts with fundamental and basics of Python programming with examples , followed by use of Modules and packages with numerical methods and computation to handle different modeling equations for solution of engineering problems.

The statistical modeling using data mining for prediction can be learned by Genetic Algorithm and artificial neural network. Chapters 12 are all applications of real world problems. All Python codes are compiled and run by Spyder IDE. Hope this book will create interest you in Python, Computer Modeling and AI. It will also solve all your difficulties and boost your career

Authors   September 2023
S Paul ,R Paul, C Paul

Contents

4. **Modules and Packages**

5. **Array and File Handling**

6. **Object Oriented Programming**

Chapter 1
Why I learn Python

1.1 Introduction

In the world of programming, Python is known as one of the most popular and fastest-growing programming languages, It is an open source and globally freely distributed.

Python has huge applications in Science, Engineering, business, banking, finances, image processing and Artificial Intelligence. It is also used for machine learning to building websites and software testing. Python is used across a wide variety of industries, for building mobile, web and desktop applications. With advent of Robotics in today's world, it has new applications for building software that controls self-driving cars, automates.

Python facilitates data analysis and visualization. The rich and efficient libraries allow data processing. It helps data scientists to perform complex numeric computing operations.

1.2 Dynamic Programming

Program coding and compiling are dynamic, unlike C or Java. That is you don't have compile your program to find and rectify errors. The moment you write code , if something is wrong, it will be indicated by red mark.

In Python we are not required to declare type for variables. Whenever we are assigning the value, based on value, type will be allocated automatically. Hence Python is considered as dynamically typed language. But Java, C etc are Statically Typed Languages because we have to provide type at the beginning only.

This dynamic typing nature will provide more flexibility to the programmer.

1.3 Extensible

You can extend the functionality of Python application with the some other languages applications. It means that -

Let us assume that some C program is there, some Java program is there, can we use these applications in our Python program or not? yes, we can use other language programs in Python.

What is the need of that?

a. Suppose We want to develop a Python application, assume that some xyz functionality is required to

develop the Python application.

b. There is some java code is already there for this xyz functionality. It is non python code. Is it possible to use this non-python code in side our python application.

1.4 . Embedded

Embedded means it is same as extensible in reverse.We can use Python programs in any other language programs. i.e., we can embed Python programs anywhere.

1.5. Extensive Library

In Python for every requirement, a readymade library is available. Laths of libraries are there in Python. No other programming language has this much of library support.

Python has a rich inbuilt library.

Being a programmer we can use this library directly and we are not responsible to implement the functionality.

1.6 Good Job market

Today worldwide it has very good IT job market in the following areas

Applications	Job Market
Developing Web	Email, Online E-commerce, Facebook
Network Applications	Chatting Client-Server
Games development	Soccer, Cricket, Puzzle
Machine Learning	Data Analysis
Artificial Intelligence	Data Analysis
Neural Network	Process Optimization
Data Science	Data Analysis

Chapter 2

Install Python and IDE

2.1 Python Install

One can also install the core Python from:

https://www.python.org

It is free and open source . Please install version 3.0 +

If you open Python IDLE, it will look like as shown below.

```
IDLE Shell 3.11.4                                              —    □
File  Edit  Shell  Debug  Options  Window  Help
    Python 3.11.4 (tags/v3.11.4:d2340ef, Jun  7 2023, 05:45:37) [MSC v.1934 64 bit
    AMD64)] on win32
    Type "help", "copyright", "credits" or "license()" for more information.
>>> |
```

Both will work when you code. But the best will be Python
editors or IDE like Spyder as listed below, where you can
write and run your coder i with ease in windows like systems

2.2 Install pip

install the additional Python Package PIP.

https://pypi.org/project/pip/

Using pip, one can install additional packages and modules
as explained below. Type at command prompt

pip install **numpy**

NumPy is a module, you will use quite often, as
described in the chapter 4

2.3 Python IDE

The basic code editor, or an integrated development environment, called IDLE.

List of Python IDLE

1. Spyder

2. Jupyter Notebook

3. PyCharm

4. Visual Studio

5. Wing Python IDE

2.3.1 Spyder

Spyder is an open source cross-platform integrated development environment

(IDE) for scientific programming in the Python language.

Web: https://www.spyder-ide.org

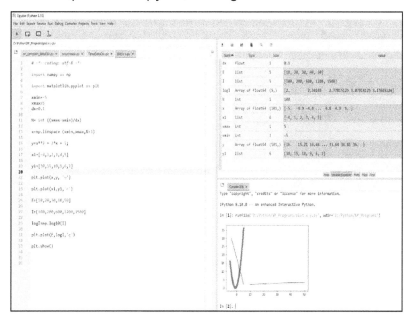

If you install Spyder and run a program, it will look like this

2.3.2 Visual Studio

Microsoft Visual Studio is an integrated development environment (IDE) from Microsoft. It is used to develop computer programs, as well as websites, web apps, web services and mobile apps. The deafult (main) programming language in Visual studio is C, but many other programming languages are supported.

Visual studio is available for Windows and macOS.

Visual Studio (from 2017), has integrated support for Python, it is called "Python Support in Visual Studio".

Web:https://visualstudio.microsoft.com

2.3.3 Jupyter Notebook will be like one shown below

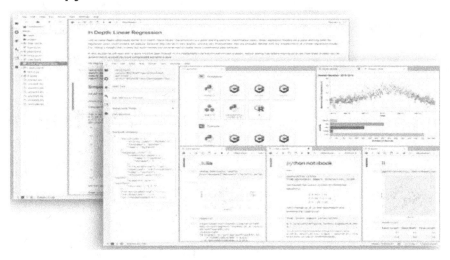

The most of the programs in this book have been edited and run by Spyder IDE.

2.4. Anaconda

Anaconda is a distribution package, where you get Python compiler, Python packages and the Spyder editor, all in one package.

Anaconda includes Python, the Jupyter Notebook, and other commonly used packages for python

They offer a free version (Anaconda Distribution)

Web: https://www.anaconda.com

Using Anaconda, as shown below one can stall any module and package.

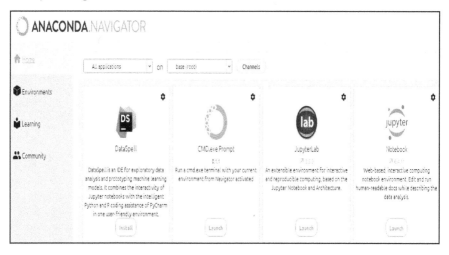

.

Chapter 3
Python Basics

3.1 Python operators

OPERATION	WHAT IT RETURNS
x + y	Sum of x and y
x - y	Difference of x and y
-x	Changed sign of x
+x	Identity of x
x * y	Product of x and y
x / y	Quotient of x and y
x // y	Quotient from floor division of x and y
x % y	Remainder of x / y
x ** y	x to the y power

3.2 Python Identifiers

A name in Python program is called identifier. It can be class name or function name or module name or variable name.

Eg: a = 20

It is a valid Python statement. Here 'a' is an identifier

Rules to define identifiers in Python:

1. The only allowed characters in Python are

alphabet symbols(either lower case or upper case)

digits(0 to 9)

underscore symbol(_)

2. Identifier should not starts with digit

3. Identifiers are case sensitive. Of course Python language itself is case sensitive language.

4. There is no length limit for Python identifiers. But not recommended to use too lengthy identifiers.

3.3 Reserved words (or) Keywords in Python

In Python some words are reserved to represent some meaning or functionality. Such type of words are calledReserved words.

There are 33 reserved words available in Python.

Python 33 keywords

['False', 'None', 'True', 'and', 'as', 'assert', 'async', 'await', 'break',

'class', 'continue', 'def', 'del', 'elif', 'else', 'except', 'finally', 'for', 'from', 'global', 'if', 'import', 'in', 'is', 'lambda', 'nonlocal', 'not', 'or', 'pass', 'raise', 'return', 'try', 'while', 'with', 'yield']

All 33 keywords contains only alphabets symbols.Except the following 3 reserved words, all contain only lower case alphabet symbols.

True

False

None

3.4 Python variables

Variables are defined with the assignment operator, \=".
Python is dynamically typed, meaning that variables can be assigned without declaring their type, unlike C or Java.

<variable name> = <value>

Example

>>> x = 3

X is a variable, no required to declare it as integer, float , string

```
# Integer
a = 2
print(a)
# Output: 2
# Floating point
pi = 3.14
print(pi)
# Output: 3.14
name = 'John Doe'
print(name)
```

Output: John Doe

Types of Variables

There are three numeric types and one text String in Python:

Int :   x = 1 # i n t

floa t :   y = 2.8

Complex : z = 3 + 2 j

Strings : 'Hello' or "Hello"

(enclosed by single ' or double " quotation

Creating variables

3.5 Data types in Python

Python contains the following in-built data types

1. int

2. float

3. complex

4. bool

5. str

6. bytes

7. bytearray

8. range

9. list

10. tuple

11. set

12. frozenset

13. dict

14. None

Example

a = 10

type(a)

Out[4]: int

Data type

1. Integer type

We can use 'int' data type to represent whole numbers (integral values

Data types: float data type

. Data types: str data type

s = 'Karthi'

print(type(s))

<class 'str'>

Convert Data to int ,float

```
x=int (input("Enter First Number:"))
y=int (input("Enter Second Number:"))
print ("The Sum:",x+y)
Enter First Number:100
Enter Second Number:200
The Sum: 300
eno=int(input("Enter Employee No:"))
ename=input("Enter Employee Name:")
esal=float(input("Enter Employee Salary:"))
eaddr=input("Enter Employee Address:")
married=bool(input("Employee Married ?[True|False]:"))
print("Please Confirm your provided Information")
```

```python
print("Employee No :",eno)
print("Employee Name :",ename)
print("Employee Salary :",esal)
print("Employee Address :",eaddr)
print("Employee Married ? :",married)
```

Enter Employee No:874578

Enter Employee Name:Karthi

Enter Employee Salary:23500

Enter Employee Address:Nandyal

Employee Married ?[True|False]:T

Please Confirm your provided Information

Employee No : 874578

Employee Name : Karthi

Employee Salary : 23500.0

Employee Address : Nandyal

Employee Married ? : True

print() without any argument

Just it prints new line character (i.e.,\n)

3.6 Python Logical Operators

Programming Loops and conditional operator

3.6.1 for Loops

A For loop is used for iterating over a sequence

```python
for i in range(5):
    .......... # equations or statements
    print(i)
```

```
for x in range(1, 6):
    ......... # equations or statements
   print(x)
```

Example Using For Loops for Summation of Data

```
data = [1, 5, 6, 3, 12, 3]

sum = 0

#Find the Sum of all the numbers
for x in data:
   sum = sum + x

print(sum)
```

3.6.2 if and else

```
number = 5
if number > 2:
print("Number is bigger than 2.")
elif number < 2: # Optional clause (you can have multiple elifs)
print("Number is smaller than 2.")
else: # Optional clause (you can only have one else)
print("Number is 2.")
```

3.6.3 IF-Else

Using If - Else:

```
a = 5
b = 8

if a > b:
    print("a is greater than b")
else:
    print("b is greater than a or a and b are equal")
```

3.6.4 Elif

Using Elif:

```
a = 5
b = 8

if a > b:
    print("a is greater than b")
elif b > a:
    print("b is greater than a")
elif a == b:
    print("a is equal to b")
```

3.7 Python Function

While creating functions we can use 2 keywords:

1. def (mandatory)

2. return (optional)

```
def function_name(argument_1, argument_
    '''
    Descriptive String
    '''

    # comments about the statements
    function_statements

    return output_parameters (optional)
```

Example

```
def squareIt(number):
print("The Square of",number,"is", number*number)
squareIt(4)
squareIt(5)
squareIt(7)
```

The Square of 4 is 16

The Square of 5 is 25

The Square of 7 is 49

Types of Functions

Python supports 2 types of functions:

1. Built in Functions

2. User Defined Functions

3.7.1 Built in Functions

The functions which are coming along with Python software automatically, are called **built in functions** or **pre defined functions**.

Eg: id(), type(), input(), eval() etc..

3.7.2 Syntax to create user defined functions:

def function_name(parameters) :

Stmt 1

Stmt 2

Stmt n

return value

Note:

Example 1

```
def calculate(a,b):
print('The Sum : ', a + b)
print('The  Difference  :  ',  a  -  b)  # Function  'calculate()'
executes 3 times
print('The Product : ', a * b)
def splog(a,b):
    value=math.log(a,b)
    print(value)
a = 20
b = 10
calculate(a,b) # Function call
a = 200
b = 100
calculate(a,b)
a = 2000
b = 1000
```

calculate(a,b)

Results

The Sum : 30

The Difference : 10

The Product : 200

The Sum : 300

The Difference : 100

The Product : 20000

The Sum : 3000

The Difference : 1000

The Product : 2000000

Example 2

```python
import math
# math.log(value,base)
a = 8
b = 4
def add(a,b): # Use Editplus editor
   sum=a+b
   print(sum)

def multiply(a,b):
    product=a*b
    print(product)

def splog(a,b):
    value=math.log(a,b)
    print(value)

x=10
y=20

print("add",x,y)
print (add(x,y))
print("multiply=",x,y)
print (multiply(x,y))
print("log=",x,y)
print(splog(x,y))
```

Output

add 10 20   30

multiply= 10 20   200

log= 10 20   0.768621786840241

Example 3

Python program to return multiple values at a time using a return statement.

```python
def calc(a,b): # Here, 'a' & 'b' are called positional arguments
sum = a + b
sub = a - b
mul = a * b
div = a / b
return sum,sub,mul,div
a,b,c,d = calc(100,50) # Positional arguments
print(a,b,c,d)
```

Alternate Way

```python
def calc(a,b): # Positional Arguments
sum = a + b
sub = a - b
mul = a * b
div = a / b
return sum,sub,mul,div
t = calc(100,50)
for x in t:
print(x)
```

Python

We will have more examples of these in the later chapters

3.8 Python Maths

3.8.1 Power , Exponential and Log

```python
a, b = 2, 3
(a ** b) # = 8
pow(a, b) # = 8
```

```python
import math
math.pow(a, b)
# output = 8.0
```

The function math.sqrt(x) calculates the square root of x.

```python
import math
import cmath
c = 4
math.sqrt(c) # = 2.0
```

```python
import math
x = 8
math.pow(x, 1/3) # evaluates to 2.0
x**(1/3) # evaluates to 2.0
```

The function math.exp(x) computes e ** x.

```python
math.exp(0) # 1.0
math.exp(1) # 2.718281828459045 (e)
```

The function math.expm1(x) computes e ** x - 1. When x is small, this gives significantly better precision than math.exp(x) - 1.

```python
math.expm1(0) # 0.0
math.exp(1e-6) - 1 # 1.0000004999621837e-06
math.expm1(1e-6) # 1.0000005000001665e-06
# exact result # 1.00000050000016666708333341666
math.log(5) # = 1.6094379124341003
# optional base argument. Default is math.e
math.log(5, math.e) # = 1.6094379124341003
```

cmath.log(5) # = *(1.6094379124341003+0j)*

math.log(1000, 10) # *3.0 (always returns float)*

cmath.log(1000, 10) # *(3+0j)*

3.8.2 Trigonometric Functions

```
import math as mt

x = 2*mt.pi

y = mt.sin(x)
print(y)

y = mt.cos(x)
print(y)

y = mt.tan(x)
print(y)
```

3.8.3 Statistics

```
import statistics as st
data = [ 1.0 , 2 . 5 , 3 . 2 5 , 5 . 7 5 ]
#Mean or Average
m = st.mean( data )
print (m)
# Standard Deviation
s t_de v = st.stdev ( data )
print ( stdev )
# Median
med = s t . median ( data )
print (med)
# Variance
```

```
var = st.variance ( data )
print ( var )
```

Statistics

Mean or average:

The mean is the sum of the data divided by the number of
data points. It is commonly called \the average

```
import  statistics  as  st
data  =  [ − 1.0 ,  2.5 ,  3.25 ,  5.75 ]

#Mean  or  Average
m  =  st . mean ( data )
print (m)

# Standard  Deviation
st_dev  =  st . stdev ( data )
print ( st_dev )

# Median
med  =  st . median ( data )
print (med)

# Variance
var  =  st . variance ( data )
print ( var )
```

```
import numpy as np

data = [-1.0,  2.5,  3.25,  5.75]

#Mean or Average
m = np.mean(data)
print(m)

# Standard Deviation
st_dev = np.std(data)
print(st_dev)

# Median
med = np.median(data)
print(med)

# Minimum Value
minv = np.min(data)
print(minv)

# Maximum Value
maxv = np.max(data)
print(maxv)
```

We can also write it like this:

```
import math as mt

x = 3.14

y = mt.sin( x )

print ( y )
```

3.8.4 Simple interest Python

```
principle=float(input("Enter the principle amount:"))

time=int(input("Enter the time(years):"))

rate=float(input("Enter the rate:"))

simple_interest=(principle*time*rate)/100

print("The simple interest is:",simple_interest)
```

Output

Enter the principle amount: 1200

Enter the time(years):10

Enter the rate:5.25

The simple interest is: 630.0

3.8.5 Compute the Student Grade

Average Mark	Grade
91-100	A1
81-90	A2
71-80	B1
61-70	B2
51-60	C1
41-50	C2
33-40	D
21-32	E1
0-20	E2

Program

```
print("Enter Marks Obtained in 5 Subjects: ")
markOne = int(input())
markTwo = int(input())
markThree = int(input())
markFour = int(input())
markFive = int(input())
tot = markOne+markTwo+markThree+markFour+markFive
avg = tot/5
if avg>=91 and avg<=100:
    print("Your Grade is A1")
elif avg>=81 and avg<91:
    print("Your Grade is A2")
elif avg>=71 and avg<81:
    print("Your Grade is B1")
elif avg>=61 and avg<71:
    print("Your Grade is B2")
elif avg>=51 and avg<61:
    print("Your Grade is C1")
elif avg>=41 and avg<51:
    print("Your Grade is C2")
elif avg>=33 and avg<41:
    print("Your Grade is D")
elif avg>=21 and avg<33:
    print("Your Grade is E1")
elif avg>=0 and avg<21:
    print("Your Grade is E2")
else:
    print("Invalid Input!")
```

print("Enter Marks Obtained in 5 Subjects: ")

markOne = int(input())

markTwo = int(input())

markThree = int(input())

markFour = int(input())

markFive = int(input())

```python
tot = markOne+markTwo+markThree+markFour+markFive
avg = tot/5

if avg>=91 and avg<=100:
    print("Your Grade is A1")
elif avg>=81 and avg<91:
    print("Your Grade is A2")
elif avg>=71 and avg<81:
    print("Your Grade is B1")
elif avg>=61 and avg<71:
    print("Your Grade is B2")
elif avg>=51 and avg<61:
    print("Your Grade is C1")
elif avg>=41 and avg<51:
    print("Your Grade is C2")
elif avg>=33 and avg<41:
    print("Your Grade is D")
elif avg>=21 and avg<33:
    print("Your Grade is E1")
elif avg>=0 and avg<21:
    print("Your Grade is E2")
else:
    print("Invalid Input!")
```

Output

Enter Marks Obtained in 5 Subjects:

67

90

71

54

61

3.9 Python Graphics

Graphics require a module called, Matplotlib , a Python 2D plotting library which produces publication-quality figures in a variety of hardcopy formats

Example Python code

```
import matplotlib.pyplot as plt
x = [1,2,3,4]
y = [10,20,25,30]
fig = plt.figure()
ax = fig.add_subplot(111)
ax.plot(x, y, color='blue', linewidth=3)
ax.scatter([2,4,6], [5,15,25],color='red',
marker='^')
ax.set_xlim(1, 6.5)
plt.savefig('foo.png')
plt.show()
```

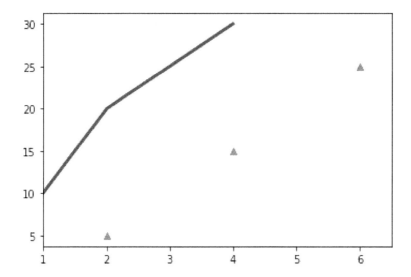

```
import matplotlib.pyplot as plt
import numpy as np
xmin=-5
xmax=5
dx=0.1

N= int ((xmax-xmin)/dx)

x=np.linspace (xmin,xmax,N+1)

y=x**2 + 2*x + 1;

x1=[-4,1,2,3,4,5]

y1=[30,15,10,9,6,2]

plt.plot(x,y, 'o')

plt.plot(x1,y1,'r')

E=[10,20,30,40,50]

I=[100,200,600,1200,1500]

logI=np.log10(I)
plt.plot(E,logI,'g')
plt.show()
```

Your Grade is B2

3.10 Conversion Decimal- Binary-Decimal

3.10.1 Decimal to Binary

```
print("Enter the Decimal Number: ")
dnum = int(input())
i = 0
bnum = []
while dnum!=0:
    rem = dnum%2
    bnum.insert(i, rem)
    i = i+1
    dnum = int(dnum/2)

i = i-1
print("\nEquivalent Binary Value is:")
while i>=0:
    print(end=str(bnum[i]))
    i = i-1
print()
```

print("Enter the Decimal Number: ")

dnum = int(input())

i = 0

bnum = []

while dnum!=0:

  rem = dnum%2

  bnum.insert(i, rem)

  i = i+1

  dnum = int(dnum/2)

```python
    i = i-1
print("\nEquivalent Binary Value is:")
while i>=0:
    print(end=str(bnum[i]))
    i = i-1
print()
```

output

Enter the Decimal Number: 22

Equivalent Binary Value is: 10110

3.10.2 Binary to Decimal

```python
print("Enter the Binary Number: ")
bnum = int(input())

dnum = 0
i = 1
while bnum!=0:
    rem = bnum%10
    dnum = dnum + (rem*i)
    i = i*2
    bnum = int(bnum/10)
```

print("\nEquivalent Decimal Value = ", dnum)


```
print("Enter the Binary Number: ")
bnum = int(input())

dnum = 0
i = 1
while bnum!=0:
    rem = bnum%10
    dnum = dnum + (rem*i)
    i = i*2
    bnum = int(bnum/10)

print("\nEquivalent Decimal Value = ", dnum)
```

Output

Enter the Binary Number: 10011

Equivalent Decimal Value = 19

Chapter 4
Modules and Packages

4.1 Introduction

In Python, both modules and packages organize and structure the code but serve different purposes. In simple terms, a module is a single file containing python code, whereas a package is a collection of modules that are organized in a directory hierarchy.

Advantages of Modules

1. Code Reusability
2. Readability improved
3. Maintainability improved

4.2 Built in Modules

List of Modules

NumPy - NumPy is the fundamental package   for scientific computing with Python
library: http://www.numpy.org

SciPy - SciPy is a free and open-source Python library used for scientific computing and technical computing. SciPy contains modules for optimiza- tion, linear algebra, integration, interpolation, special functions, FFT, sig- nal and image processing, ODE solvers and other tasks common in science and engineering.

library: http://www.scipy.org

Matplotlib - Matplotlib is a Python 2D plotting library
library: http://www.matplotlib.org
Following Plotting functions that you will use a lot under
this module: plot(), title(), xlabel(), ylabel(), axis(),
grid(),subplot(), legend(), show()

Math – for all mathematical functions like log, expotential
trigonometry, Sin, Cos etc

Statistics – To find out mean mode, standard deviation etc
of statistical data

TensorFlow
It is **a Python library for fast numerical computing
created and released by Google**. It is a foundation library
that can be used to create Deep Learning models directly or
by using wrapper libraries that simplify the process built on
top of TensorFlow. TensorFlow is an end-to-end open
source platform for **machine learning**. TensorFlow is a rich
system for managing all aspects of a machine learning
system
MNIST

MNIST set is **a large collection of handwritten digits**. It is a very popular dataset in the field of image processing. It is often used for benchmarking machine learning algorithms

4.3 Make your Own Module

A module is a file containing Python definitions and statements. The file name is the module name with the suffix .py

Every Python file (.py) acts as a module.

Let us save the following code as **spmath.py**, and itself is a module

```
x = 888
y = 999
def add(a,b): # Use Editplus editor
print('The Sum : ',a+b)
def product(a,b):
print('The product :', a*b)
```

4.4 importing a module

Syntax of importing a module

import module name

We can access members by using module name.

Module name.variable

Module name.function()

Example

```
import spmath
a=23
```

b=45

spmath.add(10,20) # *Executed in Editplus editor*

spath.product(10,20)

4.5 Renaming a module at the time of import

import spmath as s

import spmath as s

v1=s.add(10,20) # *Executed in Editplus editor*

v2=s.product(10,20)

print(r.x)

print(v1,v2)

We can import particular members of module by using

from ... import.

Example

from spmath import x,add

print(x)

add(10,20)

product(10,20)

4. 6 Examples of Modules Applications

4.6.1 Math

--

from math import

x = 3.14

y = sin (x)

pr in t (y)

```
y = cos ( x )
print ( y )
```


We can also use this alternative:

```
import math
x = 3.14
y = math.sin( x )
print ( y )
```

We can also write it like this:

```
import math as mt
x = 3.14
y = mt.s i n( x )
print ( y )
```

4.6.2 Statistics

```
import  statistics as st
 data = [ 1.0 , 2 . 5 , 3 . 2 5 , 5 . 7 5 ]
#Mean or Average
 m = st.mean( data )
print (m)
# Standard Deviation
s t_de v = st.stdev ( data )
print ( stdev )
# Median
```

```python
med = s t . median ( data )
print (med)
# Variance
var = st.variance ( data )
print ( var )
```

4.6.3 Numpy

```python
import numpy as np
a = np . ar ray ( [ 1 , 3 , 7 , 2 ] )
A = np.array ( [ [ 1 , 3 , 7 , 2 ] , [ 5 , 8 , 9, 0 ] ,[ 6 , 7, 11 , 1 2 ]
] )
B= np.array ( [ [ 4 , 3 , 0 , 2 ] , [ 3 , 8 , 8, 0 ] , [ 6 , 7, 11 , 1 2
] ] )
C = A + B
D = A. dot (B)
E = A. transpose ( )
print (C)
print (D)
print (E)
```

4.6.4 Matplotlib

```
5      import matplotlib.pyplot as plt
6      import numpy as np
7      xmin=-5
8      xmax=5
9      dx=0.1
10
11     N= int ((xmax-xmin)/dx)
12
13     x=np.linspace (xmin,xmax,N+1)
14
15     y=x**2 + 2*x + 1;
16
17     x1=[-4,1,2,3,4,5]
18
19     y1=[30,15,10,9,6,2]
20
21     plt.plot(x,y, 'o')
22
23     plt.plot(x1,y1,'r')
24
25     E=[10,20,30,40,50]
26
27     I=[100,200,600,1200,1500]
28
29     logI=np.log10(I)
30
31     plt.plot(E,logI,'g')
32     |
33     plt.show()
```

Nam▲	Type	Size	Value
dx	float	1	0.1
E	list	5	[10, 20, 30, 40, 50]
I	list	5	[100, 200, 600, 1200, 1500]
logI	Array of float64	(5,)	[2. 2.30103 2.77815125 3.07918125 3.17609126]
N	int	1	100
x	Array of float64	(101,)	[-5. -4.9 -4.8 ... 4.8 4.9 5.]
x1	list	6	[-4, 1, 2, 3, 4, 5]
xmax	int	1	5
xmin	int	1	-5
y	Array of float64	(101,)	[16. 15.21 14.44 ... 33.64 34.81 36.]
y1	list	6	[30, 15, 10, 9, 6, 2]

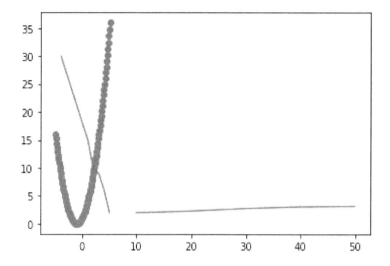

Chapter 5

Array and File Handling

5.1 Arrays

An array is a special variable, which can hold more than one value at a time. It is a collection of either homogeneous or heterogeneous elements, and may contain int, strings or other lists.

```
my_array = array('i', [1,2,3,4,5])
print(my_array[0])  # 1
print(my_array[2])  # 3
print(my_array[0])  # 1
```

Similarly data is an array.

```
data = [1.6, 3.4, 5.5, 9.4]

N = len(data)

print(N)

print(data[2])

data[2] = 7.3

print(data[2])

for x in data:
    print(x)
```

output

data = [1 . 6 , 3 . 4 , 5 . 5 , 9 . 4]

5.2 Dictionary

A dictionary is an example of a a variable with value in string **literal syntax**

d = {} # *empty dict*

d = {'key': 'value'} # *dict with initial values*

Creating and populating it with values

stock = {'eggs': 5, 'milk': 2}

Or creating an empty dictionary

dictionary = {}

And populating it after

dictionary['eggs'] = 5

dictionary['milk'] = 2

Values can also be lists

mydict = {'a': [1, 2, 3], 'b': ['one', 'two', 'three']}

dict() constructor

The dict() constructor can be used to create dictionaries from keyword arguments, or from a single iterable of

key-value pairs, or from a single dictionary and keyword arguments.

```
dict(a=1, b=2, c=3)                    # {'a': 1, 'b': 2, 'c': 3}
dict([('d', 4), ('e', 5), ('f', 6)])   # {'d': 4, 'e': 5, 'f': 6}
dict([('a', 1)], b=2, c=3)             # {'a': 1, 'b': 2, 'c': 3}
dict({'a' : 1, 'b' : 2}, c=3)          # {'a': 1, 'b': 2, 'c': 3}
```

5.3 List

The Python **List** is a general data structure widely used in Python

Starting with a given list a: a = [1, 2, 3, 4, 5]

1. append(value) – appends a new element to the end of the list.

a.append(6)

a.append(7)

a.append(7)

 # a: [1, 2, 3, 4, 5, 6, 7, 7]

2. extend(enumerable) – extends the list by appending elements from another enumerable.

a = [1, 2, 3, 4, 5, 6, 7, 7]

b = [8, 9, 10]

 # Extend list by appending all elements from b

a.extend(b)

 # a: [1, 2, 3, 4, 5, 6, 7, 7, 8, 9, 10]

 # Extend list with elements from a non-list enumerable:

a.extend(range(3))

 # a: [1, 2, 3, 4, 5, 6, 7, 7, 8, 9, 10, 0, 1, 2]

3. index(value, [startIndex]) – gets the index of the first occurrence of the input value. If the input value is not in the list a ValueError exception is raised. If a second argument is provided, the search is started at that specified index.

a.index(7)

 # Returns: 6

4. insert(index, value) – inserts value just before the specified index. Thus after the insertion the new element occupies position index.

a.insert(0, 0) # *insert 0 at position 0*

a.insert(2, 5) # *insert 5 at position 2*

a: [0, 1, 5, 2, 3, 4, 5, 6, 7, 7, 8, 9, 10]

5. pop([index]) – removes and returns the item at index. With no argument it removes and returns the last element of the list.

a.pop(2)

Returns: 5

a: [0, 1, 2, 3, 4, 5, 6, 7, 7, 8, 9, 10]

a.pop(8)

Returns: 7

a: [0, 1, 2, 3, 4, 5, 6, 7, 8, 9, 10]

With no argument:

a.pop()

Returns: 10

a: [0, 1, 2, 3, 4, 5, 6, 7, 8, 9]

6.

6. remove(value) – removes the first occurrence of the specified value. If the provided value cannot be found, a ValueError is raised.

a.remove(0)

a.remove(9)

a: [1, 2, 3, 4, 5, 6, 7, 8]

a.remove(10)

ValueError, because 10 is not in a

7. reverse() – reverses the list in-place and returns None.

a.reverse()

a: [8, 7, 6, 5, 4, 3, 2, 1]

There are also other ways of reversing a list.

8. count(value) – counts the number of occurrences of some value in the list.

a.count(7)

Returns: 2

9. sort() – sorts the list in numerical and lexicographical order and returns None.

a.sort()

a = [1, 2, 3, 4, 5, 6, 7, 8]

Sorts the list in numerical order

Lists can also be reversed when sorted using the reverse=True flag in the sort() method.

a.sort(reverse=True)

a = [8, 7, 6, 5, 4, 3, 2, 1]

If you want to sort by attributes of items, you can use the key keyword argument:

```python
import datetime

class Person(object):
    def __init__(self, name, birthday, height):
        self.name = name
        self.birthday = birthday
        self.height = height
    def __repr__(self):
        return self.name
```

```python
l = [Person("John Cena", datetime.date(1992, 9, 12), 175),
Person("Chuck Norris", datetime.date(1990, 8, 28), 180),
Person("Jon Skeet", datetime.date(1991, 7, 6), 185)]
l.sort(key=lambda item: item.name)
# l: [Chuck Norris, John Cena, Jon Skeet]
l.sort(key=lambda item: item.birthday)
# l: [Chuck Norris, Jon Skeet, John Cena]
l.sort(key=lambda item: item.height)
# l: [John Cena, Chuck Norris, Jon Skeet]
import datetime
l = [{'name':'John Cena', 'birthday': datetime.date(1992, 9,
12),'height': 175},
{'name': 'Chuck Norris', 'birthday': datetime.date(1990, 8,
28),'height': 180},
{'name': 'Jon Skeet', 'birthday': datetime.date(1991, 7, 6),
'height': 185}]
l.sort(key=lambda item: item['name'])
# l: [Chuck Norris, John Cena, Jon Skeet]
l.sort(key=lambda item: item['birthday'])
# l: [Chuck Norris, Jon Skeet, John Cena]
l.sort(key=lambda item: item['height'])
# l: [John Cena, Chuck Norris, Jon Skeet]
```

10. clear() – removes all items from the list

```python
a.clear()
# a = []
```

11. **Replication** – multiplying an existing list by an integer will produce a larger list consisting of that many copies of the original. This can be useful for example for list initialization:

```
b = ["blah"] * 3
# b = ["blah", "blah", "blah"]
```

```
b = [1, 3, 5] * 5
# [1, 3, 5, 1, 3, 5, 1, 3, 5, 1, 3, 5, 1, 3, 5]
```

Take care doing this if your list contains references to objects (eg a list of lists), see Common Pitfalls - List multiplication and common references.

12. **Element deletion** – it is possible to delete multiple elements in the list using the del keyword and slice notation:

```
a = list(range(10))
del a[::2]
# a = [1, 3, 5, 7, 9]
del a[-1]
# a = [1, 3, 5, 7]
del a[:]
# a = []
```

13. **Copying**

The default assignment "=" assigns a reference of the original list to the new name. That is, the original name and new name are both pointing to the same list object. Changes made through any of them will be reflected in another. This is often not what you intended.

b = a

a.append(6)

b: [1, 2, 3, 4, 5, 6]

If you want to create a copy of the list you have below options.

You can slice it:

new_list = old_list[:]

You can use the built in list() function:

new_list = list(old_list)

Accessing list values

Python lists are zero-indexed, and act like arrays in other languages.

lst = [1, 2, 3, 4]

lst[0] # 1

lst[1] # 2

lst[1:] # [2, 3, 4]

lst[:3] # [1, 2, 3]

lst[::2] # [1, 3]

lst[::-1] # [4, 3, 2, 1]

lst[-1:0:-1] # [4, 3, 2]

lst[5:8] # *[] since starting index is greater than length of lst,*
returns empty list
lst[1:10] # *[2, 3, 4] same as omitting ending index*

5.4 Tuple

Syntactically, a tuple is a comma-separated list of values:
it is common to enclose tuples in parentheses:

t = ('a', 'b', 'c', 'd', 'e')

t = tuple('lupins')

print(t) # *('l', 'u', 'p', 'i', 'n', 's')*

t = tuple(range(3))

print(t) # *(0, 1, 2)*

One of the main differences between lists and tuples in
Python is that tuples are immutable, that is, one cannot
add or modify items once the tuple is initialized.
Similarly, tuples don't have .append and .extend methods as
list does. Using += is possible, but it changes the
binding of the variable, and not the tuple itself:

5.5 Array Import

To use arrays in python language, you need to import the
standard array module. This is because array is not a
fundamental data type like strings, integer etc. Here is how
you can import array module in python :

```
from array import *
my_array = array('i', [1,2,3,4,5])
for i in my_array:
    print(i)
# 1    # 2    # 3   # 4   # 5
```

5.6 Append and Delete Data

Append any value to the array using append() method

```
my_array = array('i', [1,2,3,4,5])
my_array.append(6)
# array('i', [1, 2, 3, 4, 5, 6])
```

a.append(6)

a: [1, 2, 3, 4, 5, 6, 7]

Element deletion

del a[::2]

a = [1, 3, 5, 7]

5.7 Slice Data

The slice operator also works on lists:

```
>>> t = ['a', 'b', 'c', 'd', 'e', 'f']
>>> t[1:3]  # ['b', 'c']
>>> t[:4]  # ['a', 'b', 'c', 'd']
>>> t[3:] #  ['d', 'e', 'f']
```

t = ['a', 'b', 'c']

>>> t.append('d')

>>> print(t)

['a', 'b', 'c', 'd']

DELETING ELEMENTS

```
t = ['a', 'b', 'c']
>>> del t[1]
>>> print(t)
['a', 'c']
```

remove:

```
>>> t = ['a', 'b', 'c']
>>> t.remove('b')
>>> print(t)
['a', 'c']
```

To remove more than one element, you can use del with a slice index:

```
>>> t = ['a', 'b', 'c', 'd', 'e', 'f']
>>> del t[1:5]
>>> print(t)
['a', 'f']
```

5.8 Reshaping arrays

```
arr = np.array([1, 2, 3, 4, 5, 6, 7, 8, 9, 10, 11, 12])
newarr = arr.reshape(4, 3)
print(newarr)
[[ 1  2  3]
 [ 4  5  6]
 [ 7  8  9]
 [10 11 12]]
```

change to 4 rows 3 coluimns

5.9 Data Frame

```
# Convert the dictionary into DataFrame
df = pd.DataFrame(data)
df = pd.DataFrame(np.arange(12).reshape(3, 4),
          columns=['A', 'B', 'C', 'D'])
```

```
   A  B  C   D
0  0  1  2   3
1  4  5  6   7
2  8  9  10  11
```

5.9.1 Drop columns and rows

```
df.drop(columns=['B', 'C'])
```

```
   A   D
0  0   3
1  4   7
2  8  11
```

Drop a row by index

```
   A  B  C   D
0  0  1  2   3
1  4  5  6   7
2  8  9  10  11
```

```
df.drop([0, 1])
```

```
   A  B  C   D
2  8  9  10  11
```

Drop Columns from a Dataframe using **drop()** method.

```python
# Import pandas package
import pandas as pd
 # create a dictionary with five fields each
data = {
   'A': ['A1', 'A2', 'A3', 'A4', 'A5'],
   'B': ['B1', 'B2', 'B3', 'B4', 'B5'],
   'C': ['C1', 'C2', 'C3', 'C4', 'C5'],
   'D': ['D1', 'D2', 'D3', 'D4', 'D5'],
   'E': ['E1', 'E2', 'E3', 'E4', 'E5']}
 # Remove column name 'A'
df. drop(['A'], axis=1)
output
```

	B	C	D	E
0	B1	C1	D1	E1
1	B2	C2	D2	E2
2	B3	C3	D3	E3
3	B4	C4	D4	E4
4	B5	C5	D5	E5

```python
a = [1, 2, 3, 4, 5]
a.append(6)
a: [1, 2, 3, 4, 5, 6, 7]
```

Element deletion

del a[::2]

a = [1, 3, 5, 7]

The slice operator also works on lists:

```
>>> t = ['a', 'b', 'c', 'd', 'e', 'f']
>>> t[1:3]  #  ['b', 'c']
>>> t[:4]  #  ['a', 'b', 'c', 'd']
>>> t[3:] #   ['d', 'e', 'f']
```

```
t = ['a', 'b', 'c']
>>> t.append('d')
>>> print(t)
['a', 'b', 'c', 'd']
```

DELETING ELEMENTS

```
t = ['a', 'b', 'c']
>>> del t[1]
>>> print(t)
['a', 'c']
```

remove:

```
>>> t = ['a', 'b', 'c']
>>> t.remove('b')
>>> print(t)
['a', 'c']
```

To remove more than one element, you can use del with a slice index:

```
>>> t = ['a', 'b', 'c', 'd', 'e', 'f']
>>> del t[1:5]
>>> print(t)
['a', 'f']
```

Drop Columns from a Dataframe using drop() **method.**

```
# Import pandas package
import pandas as pd

# create a dictionary with five fields each
data = {
    'A': ['A1', 'A2', 'A3', 'A4', 'A5'],
    'B': ['B1', 'B2', 'B3', 'B4', 'B5'],
    'C': ['C1', 'C2', 'C3', 'C4', 'C5'],
    'D': ['D1', 'D2', 'D3', 'D4', 'D5'],
    'E': ['E1', 'E2', 'E3', 'E4', 'E5']}

# Convert the dictionary into DataFrame
df = pd.DataFrame(data)

# Remove column name 'A'
df.drop(['A'], axis=1)
output
```

	B	C	D	E
0	B1	C1	D1	E1
1	B2	C2	D2	E2
2	B3	C3	D3	E3
3	B4	C4	D4	E4
4	B5	C5	D5	E5

```
df = pd.DataFrame(np.arange(12).reshape(3, 4),
        columns=['A', 'B', 'C', 'D'])
df
```

```
  A B C  D
0 0 1 2  3
1 4 5 6  7
2 8 9 10 11
```

Drop columns
```
df.drop(columns=['B', 'C'])
```
```
  A D
0 0 3
1 4 7
2 8 11
```

Drop a row by index

```
A B  C  D
0 0 1  2  3
1 4 5  6  7
2 8 9 10 11
```

df.drop([0, 1])
```
 A B  C  D
2 8 9 10 11
```

5.10 File Handling

Python has several functions for creating, reading, updating, and deleting files. The key function for working with files in Python is the open() function.

5.10. Files Opening Modes

There are four different methods (modes) for opening a file:

"x" - Creates the specified file, returns an error if the file exists

"w" - Opens a file for writing, creates the file if it does not exist

_ "r" -. Opens a file for reading, error if the file does not exist

"a" - Append - Opens a file for appending, creates the file if it does not exist In addition you can specify if the file should be handled as binary or text mode

"t" - Text - Default value. Text mode

"b" - Binary - Binary mode (e.g. images)

'rb' - reading mode in binary. This is similar to r except that the reading is forced in binary mode. This is
also a default choice.

'r+' - reading mode plus writing mode at the same time. This allows you to read and write into files at the
same time without having to use r and w.

'rb+' - reading and writing mode in binary. The same as r+ except the data is in binary

'wb' - writing mode in binary. The same as w except the data is in binary.

'w+' - writing and reading mode. The exact same as r+ but if the file does not exist, a new one is made.
Otherwise, the file is overwritten.

'wb+' - writing and reading mode in binary mode. The same as w+ but the data is in binary.

'ab' - appending in binary mode. Similar to a except that the data is in binary.

'a+' - appending and reading mode. Similar to w+ as it will create a new file if the file does not exist.
Otherwise, the file pointer is at the end of the file if it exists.

'ab+' - appending and reading mode in binary. The same as a+ except that the data is in binary.

with open(filename, 'r') as f:
f.read()
with open(filename, 'w') as f:

```
f.write(filedata)
```

with open(filename, 'a') as f:

```
f.write('\\n' + newdata)
```

	r	r+	w	w+	a	a+
Read	✔	✔	✗	✔	✗	✔
Write	✗	✔	✔	✔	✔	✔
Creates file	✗	✗	✔	✔	✔	✔
Erases file	✗	✗	✔	✔	✗	✗
Initial position	Start	Start	Start	Start	End	End

GoalKicker.com – Python® Notes for Professionals 172

Python

5.11 Reading and Writing Data from Files

5.11.1 Reading a file line-by-line

The simplest way to iterate over a file line-by-line:

```python
with open('myfile.txt', 'r') as fp:
    for line in fp:
        print(line)
```

`readline()` allows for more granular control above:

```python
with open('myfile.txt', 'r') as fp:
    while True:
        cur_line = fp.readline()
# If the result is an empty string
if cur_line == '':
    # We have reached the end of the file
    break
print(cur_line)
```

5.11.2 Open CSV file and read data

```python
import numpy as np
import csv

CSVData = open("data1.csv")
Array2d_result = np.loadtxt(CSVData, delimiter=",")
print(Array2d_result)


csv_filename = 'data1.csv'
with open(csv_filename) as f:
    reader = csv.reader(f)
    p= list(reader)
    print(p)
```

	A	B	C
1	15	3	7
2	15	2.5	7
3	15	2	7
4	15	1.5	7
5	15	0.8	7
6	17	0.8	7
7	19	0.8	7
8	21	0.8	7
9	23	0.8	7
10	24	0.8	7

```
[[15.    3.    7. ]
 [15.    2.5   7. ]
 [15.    2.    7. ]
 [15.    1.5   7. ]
 [15.    0.8   7. ]
 [17.    0.8   7. ]
 [19.    0.8   7. ]
 [21.    0.8   7. ]
 [23.    0.8   7. ]
 [24.    0.8   7. ]]
```

5.11.3 Reading CSV excel file using pandas

import pandas as pd

p= pd.read_csv('inp.csv', index_col = [0])

print(p)

This is inv.csv file

	A	B	C	D	E
1	15	3.4	0.14	0.5	7
2	15	3	0.14	0.5	7
3	15	2.5	0.14	0.5	7
4	15	2	0.14	0.5	7
5	15	1.5	0.14	0.5	7
6	15	0.8	0.14	0.5	7
7	17	0.8	0.14	0.5	7
8	19	0.8	0.14	0.5	7
9	21	0.8	0.14	0.5	7
10	23	0.8	0.14	0.5	7

This is output

```
15   3.4   0.14   0.5   7
15   3.0   0.14   0.5   7
15   2.5   0.14   0.5   7
15   2.0   0.14   0.5   7
15   1.5   0.14   0.5   7
15   0.8   0.14   0.5   7
17   0.8   0.14   0.5   7
19   0.8   0.14   0.5   7
21   0.8   0.14   0.5   7
23   0.8   0.14   0.5   7
```

5.11.4 Reading excel file and Graphics Data

```python
import matplotlib.pyplot as plt

import pandas as pd

file = pd.read_excel('data.xlsx')

x_axis = file['X values']

y_axis = file['Y values']

plt.bar(x_axis, y_axis, width=5)

plt.xlabel("X-Axis")

plt.ylabel("Y-Axis")

plt.show()
```

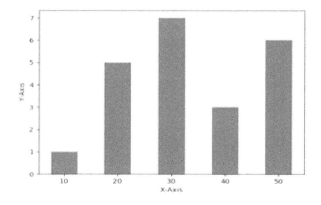

import matplotlib.pyplot as plt

```
import pandas as pd
file = pd.read_excel('data.xlsx')
plt.pie(file['Value'],labels=file['Label'])
plt.show()
```

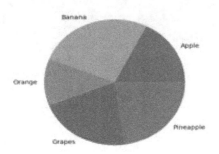

5.11.5 Use Open() function reading file

Another way to read file with open () function

```
import numpy as np
import csv
CSVData = open("data1.csv")
Array2d_result = np.loadtxt(CSVData, delimiter=",")
print(Array2d_result)
csv_filename = 'data1.csv'
with open(csv_filename) as f:
    reader = csv.reader(f)
    p= list(reader)
    print(p)
```

Open a data file and plot graph using it

```
import matplotlib.pyplot as plt
```

```python
import csv
E = [ ]
I = [ ]
with open('EI_CV.csv','r') as csvfile:
    lines = csv.reader(csvfile, delimiter=',')
    for row in lines:
        print( E.append(row[0]))
        print(I.append(int(row[1])))
plt.plot(E, I, color = 'g', linestyle = 'dashed',
         marker = 'o',label = "E I Data")
plt.xticks(rotation = 25)
plt.xlabel('E Potential mV')
plt.ylabel('Current Density mA/cm2')
plt.title('CV Battery', fontsize = 20)
plt.grid()
plt.legend()
plt.show()
```

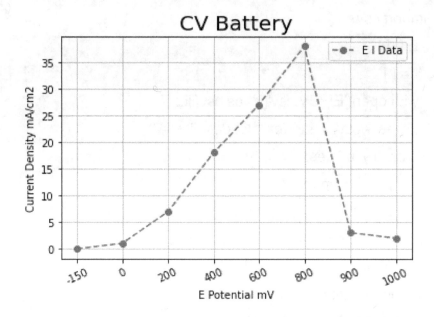

CV Battery

5.11.6 Read input and output files inv.csv and opt.csv

```
import matplotlib.pyplot as plt
import pandas as pd

inp_file =pd.read_csv("inp.csv", sep = ';',index_col = [0])

opt_file=pd.read_csv("opt.csv", sep = ';',index_col = [0])

print(inp_file)

print(opt_file)

p=[[15,3,0.14,0.5,7],
   [15,2.5,0.14,0.5,7],
   [15,2,0.14,0.5,7],
   [15,1.5,0.14,0.5,7],
   [15,0.8,0.14,0.5,7],
   [17,0.8,0.14,0.5,7],
   [19,0.8,0.14,0.5,7],
   [21,0.8,0.14,0.5,7],
   [23,0.8,0.14,0.5,7],
   [24,0.8,0.14,0.5,7]]

t=[[19.23], [21.48], [23.97], [25.98], [28.32], [30.17], [33.45], [37.78], [39.83]
```

5.11.7 Write Data to a File

```
f = open("myfile.txt", "x")

data = "Helo World"

f.write(data)

f.close()
```

Read Data from a File

```
f = open("myfile.txt", "r")

data = f.read()

print(data)

f.close()
```

5.11.8 Logging Data to File

```
data = [1.6, 3.4, 5.5, 9.4]

f = open("myfile.txt", "x")

for value in data:
    record = str(value)
    f.write(record)
    f.write("\n")

f.close()
```

Read Logged Data from File

```
f = open("myfile.txt", "r")

for record in f:
    record = record.replace("\n", "")
    print(record)

f.close()
```

```python
# import pandas with shortcut 'pd'
import pandas as pd


# read_csv function which is used to read the required CSV
file
data = pd.read_csv('input.csv')


# display
print("Original 'input.csv' CSV Data: \n")
print(data)


# drop function which is used in removing or deleting rows
or columns from the CSV files
data.drop('year', inplace=True, axis=1)


# display
print("\nCSV Data after deleting the column 'year':\n")
print(data)
```

Original 'input.csv' CSV Data:

	id	day	month	year	item_quantity	Name
0	1	12	3	2020	12	Oliver
1	2	13	3	2020	45	Henry
2	3	14	3	2020	8	Benjamin
3	4	15	3	2020	23	John
4	5	16	3	2020	31	Camili
5	6	17	3	2020	40	Rheana
6	7	18	3	2020	55	Joseph
7	8	19	3	2020	13	Raj
8	9	20	3	2020	29	Elias
9	10	21	3	2020	19	Emily

CSV Data after deleting the column 'year':

	id	day	month	item_quantity	Name
0	1	12	3	12	Oliver
1	2	13	3	45	Henry
2	3	14	3	8	Benjamin
3	4	15	3	23	John
4	5	16	3	31	Camili
5	6	17	3	40	Rheana
6	7	18	3	55	Joseph
7	8	19	3	13	Raj
8	9	20	3	29	Elias
9	10	21	3	19	Emily

5.12 Examples Data Array File

Dropping a Column from excel

Original 'input.csv' CSV Data:

	id	day	month	year	item_quantity	Name
0	1	12	3	2020	12	Oliver
1	2	13	3	2020	45	Henry
2	3	14	3	2020	8	Benjamin
3	4	15	3	2020	23	John
4	5	16	3	2020	31	Camili
5	6	17	3	2020	40	Rheana
6	7	18	3	2020	55	Joseph
7	8	19	3	2020	13	Raj
8	9	20	3	2020	29	Elias
9	10	21	3	2020	19	Emily

```
# read_csv function which is used to read the required
CSV file
data = pd.read_csv('input.csv')
print("Original 'input.csv' CSV Data: \n")
print(data)
# pop function which is used in removing or deleting
columns from the CSV files
data.pop('year')
# display
print("\nCSV Data after deleting the column 'year':\n")
print(data)
```

	id	day	month	item_quantity	Name
0	1	12	3	12	Oliver
1	2	13	3	45	Henry
2	3	14	3	8	Benjamin
3	4	15	3	23	John
4	5	16	3	31	Camili
5	6	17	3	40	Rheana
6	7	18	3	55	Joseph
7	8	19	3	13	Raj
8	9	20	3	29	Elias
9	10	21	3	19	Emily

Here, a simple CSV file is used i.e; **input.csv**

id	day	month	year	item_quantity	Name
1	12	3	2020	12	Oliver
2	13	3	2020	45	Henry
3	14	3	2020	8	Benjamin
4	15	3	2020	23	John
5	16	3	2020	31	Camili
6	17	3	2020	40	Rheana
7	18	3	2020	55	Joseph
8	19	3	2020	13	Raj
9	20	3	2020	29	Elias
10	21	3	2020	19	Emily

```
# import pandas with shortcut 'pd'
import pandas as pd
```

```python
# read_csv function which is used to read the required CSV
file
data = pd.read_csv('input.csv')

# display
print("Original 'input.csv' CSV Data: \n")
print(data)

# drop function which is used in removing or deleting rows
or columns from the CSV files
data.drop('year', inplace=True, axis=1)

# display
print("\nCSV Data after deleting the column 'year':\n")
print(data)
```

```
Original 'input.csv' CSV Data:

   id  day  month  year  item_quantity      Name
0   1   12      3  2020             12    Oliver
1   2   13      3  2020             45     Henry
2   3   14      3  2020              8  Benjamin
3   4   15      3  2020             23      John
4   5   16      3  2020             31    Camili
5   6   17      3  2020             40    Rheana
6   7   18      3  2020             55    Joseph
7   8   19      3  2020             13       Raj
8   9   20      3  2020             29     Elias
9  10   21      3  2020             19     Emily


CSV Data after deleting the column 'year':

   id  day  month  item_quantity      Name
0   1   12      3             12    Oliver
1   2   13      3             45     Henry
2   3   14      3              8  Benjamin
3   4   15      3             23      John
4   5   16      3             31    Camili
5   6   17      3             40    Rheana
6   7   18      3             55    Joseph
7   8   19      3             13       Raj
8   9   20      3             29     Elias
9  10   21      3             19     Emily
```

5.13 Map MinMax

```python
import pandas as pd
from sklearn.preprocessing import MinMaxScaler

# load the dataset
dataframe = pd.read_csv('data.csv', usecols=[0,1,2,3,4,5], engine='python'
dataset = dataframe.values
dataset = dataset.astype('float32')
print(" Cl   SO4   O   CO3   pH   Icorr")
print(dataset)
# normalize the dataset
scaler = MinMaxScaler(feature_range=(0, 1))
dataset = scaler.fit_transform(dataset)
print("data 0-1")
print("Cl        SO4        O        CO3        pH        Icorr")
print(dataset)
# split into train and test sets
train_size = int(len(dataset) * 0.67)
test_size = len(dataset) - train_size
train, test = dataset[0:train_size,:], dataset[train_size:len(dataset),:]
print(len(train), len(test))
```

import pandas as pd

from sklearn.preprocessing import MinMaxScaler

load the dataset

dataframe = pd.read_csv('data.csv', usecols=[0,1,2,3,4,5],

engine='python')

dataset = dataframe.values

dataset = dataset.astype('float32')

print(" Cl SO4   O   CO3   pH   Icorr")

print(dataset)

```
# normalize the dataset
scaler = MinMaxScaler(feature_range=(0, 1))
dataset = scaler.fit_transform(dataset)
print("data 0-1")
print("Cl      SO4      O      CO3      pH      Icorr")
print(dataset)
# split into train and test sets
train_size = int(len(dataset) * 0.67)
test_size = len(dataset) - train_size
train, test = dataset[0:train_size,:], dataset[train_size:len(dataset),:]
print(len(train), len(test))
```

Output before Minmax operation

```
   Cl      SO4        O      CO3      pH      Icorr
[[15.      3.      0.22     1.       8.      17.23]
 [18.      2.5     0.22     0.5      7.      19.23]
 [17.      2.      0.22     0.8      9.      21.48]
 [19.      1.5     0.22     0.8      9.      23.97]
 [16.      0.8     0.22     0.8      9.      25.98]
 [17.      1.      0.22     0.8      9.      28.32]
 [19.      1.2     0.22     0.8      9.      30.17]
 [21.      1.3     0.22     0.8      9.      33.45]
 [23.      0.9     0.2      0.8      9.      37.78]
 [24.      1.      0.17     0.8      9.      39.83]
 [24.      1.3     0.24     0.8      9.      41.19]
 [24.      1.5     0.24     0.8      9.      42.23]
 [24.      1.8     0.24     0.8      8.5     44.57]
 [24.      1.1     0.24     0.8      9.      47.23]
 [24.      1.      0.24     0.8      9.      48.32]
 [24.      1.5     0.24     0.8      9.      46.21]
 [24.      2.      0.24     0.8      9.      44.67]
 [24.      3.      0.24     0.8      9.      41.79]
 [24.      3.4     0.24     0.8      8.5     39.92]
 [23.      3.4     0.24     0.8      9.      37.75]
 [21.      3.4     0.24     0.8      9.      35.12]
 [19.      3.4     0.24     0.8      9.      33.87]
 [17.      3.4     0.24     0.8      9.      30.23]
 [14.      3.4     0.24     0.8      9.      28.12]
 [18.      3.4     0.24     0.8      9.      26.07]]
```

After MinMax Operation

Cl	SO4	O	CO3	pH	Icorr
[[0.10000002	0.84615374	0.71428585	1.	0.5	0.]
[0.4000001	0.6538461|4	0.71428585	0.	0.	0.06432939]
[0.30000007	0.46153843	0.71428585	0.6	1.	0.13669991]
[0.5	0.26923072	0.71428585	0.6	1.	0.21678996]
[0.20000005	0.	0.71428585	0.6	1.	0.28144097]
[0.30000007	0.07692307	0.71428585	0.6	1.	0.35670632]
[0.5	0.15384617	0.71428585	0.6	1.	0.416211]
[0.70000017	0.19230765	0.71428585	0.6	1.	0.52171123]
[0.9	0.03846154	0.42857146	0.6	1.	0.66098416]
[1.0000001	0.07692307	0.	0.6	1.	0.7269219]
[1.0000001	0.19230765	1.	0.6	1.	0.77066576]
[1.0000001	0.26923072	1.	0.6	1.	0.8041171]
[1.0000001	0.38461536	1.	0.6	0.75	0.8793824]
[1.0000001	0.11538461	1.	0.6	1.	0.9649404]
[1.0000001	0.07692307	1.	0.6	1.	1.]
[1.0000001	0.26923072	1.	0.6	1.	0.9321325]
[1.0000001	0.46153843	1.	0.6	1.	0.8825989]
[1.0000001	0.84615374	1.	0.6	1.	0.7899647]
[1.0000001	1.	1.	0.6	0.75	0.72981656]
[0.9	1.	1.	0.6	1.	0.6600193]
[0.70000017	1.	1.	0.6	1.	0.5754261]
[0.5	1.	1.	0.6	1.	0.53522027]
[0.30000007	1.	1.	0.6	1.	0.4181409]
[0.	1.	1.	0.6	1.	0.35027343]
[0.4000001	1.	1.	0.6	1.	0.2843358]]

Chapter 6
Object Oriented Programming

6.1 What is Object Oriented Programming (OOP)

It is based on class and object. It is better to understand the object and class by practical example rather than definition and description.

- Planet is a class, Jupiter is an object
- Student is a class, engineering student is an object
- Bird is a class , parrot is a object.

. .

So an object is an entity , it has a state and behavior. Class is a group of objects which have common properties. The object and class has been explained in a schematic diagram in fig 6.1

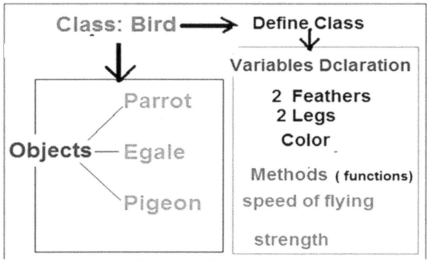

Fig 1.3 Schematic diagram illustrating Class and Object

Python is an object oriented programming (OOP) language

6.2 init () Function

For object oriented programming(OOP), described in chapter 5, all classes have a built-in function called init (), which is always executed when the class is being initiated. In C languages this is called a Constructor

6.3 self () function

The self is used **to represent the instance of the class**. With this keyword, you can access the attributes and methods of the class in python. It binds the attributes with the given arguments.

6.4 Examples

6.4.1 Car

```
# Defining the Class Car
class Car:
    def __init__(self, model, color):
        self.model = model
        self.color = color

    def displayCar(self):
        print(self.model)
        print(self.color)


# Lets start using the Class

car1 = Car("Tesla", "Red")

car1.displayCar()


car2 = Car("Ford", "Green")

print(car2.model)
print(car2.color)


car3 = Car("Volvo", "Blue")

print(car3.model)
print(car3.color)

car3.color="Black"

car3.displayCar()
```

6.4.2 Bank Account

```python
class BankAccount(object):
    defaultAccNumber = 1          # Class Attribute

    def __init__(self, name, balance = 0):
        self.name = name
        self.balance = balance
        self.accountNumber = BankAccount.defaultAccNumber
        BankAccount.defaultAccNumber = BankAccount.defaultAccNumber + 1

    def deposit(self, amount):
        self.balance += amount

    def withdraw(self, amount):
        if self.balance < amount:
            print('Not enough balance!')
        else:
            self.balance -= amount

    def getBalance(self):
        return self.balance

if __name__ == '__main__':
    myObj = BankAccount('Omkar', 1000)
    myObj.deposit(1000)
    print(myObj.getBalance())
    myObj.withdraw(500)
    print(myObj.getBalance())
```

Output

2000

1500

Chapter 7
Modeling and Simulation

7.1 Modeling

Modeling is a way of simplifying the real world to enable us to solve problems. We do it all the time and so easily that we don't even notice we are doing it. For example, a street directory is a model of a city's roads, a diagram is a model of how something is made, and even a calendar is a model of a month. Modeling is the development of an analytical structure to represent a complex system in order that the behavior of the system can be imitated and predicted. A model should be a close approximation to the real system and incorporate most of its salient features. On the other hand, it should not be so complex that it is impossible to understand and experiment with it. A good model is a judicious trade off between realism and simplicity.

3.1.1 Mathematical modeling

A mathematical model can be broadly defined as a formulation or equation that expresses the essential features of a physical system or process in mathematical terms. It is the formulation of some process or phenomenon by a set of algebraic or differential equations. The scope of the model depends on its objective , which may be process analysis, process control, process design or process optimization.

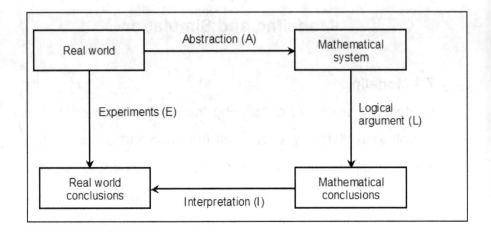

Fig 7.1 Schematic diagram for understanding of mathematical model

In a very general sense, it can be represented as a functional relationship of the form

Dependent variable = f(independent variables , parameters, influencing functions)

where the *dependent variable* is a characteristic that usually reflects the behavior or state of the system; the *independent variables* are usually dimensions, such as time and space, along which the system's behavior is being determined; the *parameters* are reflective of the system's properties or composition; and the *influencing functions* are external influences acting upon the system.

The actual mathematical expression of Eq. ( ) can range from a simple algebraic relationship to large complicated sets of differential equations.

For example consider the following reaction

$$A+B=C \qquad (7.1)$$

If we want to mathematically represent the amount of C produced (m_c) at a temperature T and pressure P in time t,

$$m_C = f (t, a_A, a_B, a_c, T, P) \qquad (7.2)$$

t is the Independent variable, the activities or concentration $a_A, a_B, a_c,$ T & P are influencing function which depend on other external factors.

7.2 Types of modelling

There are different techniques of models developments, Empirical, Semi-empirical and Rational

1. Empirical (Statistical), where data obtained from laboratory and plant are fitted with some equation by statistical regression analysis.

2. Semi-empirical, which is partly based on theory and partly on empirical data; dimensionless correlation come under this category.

3.Rational (theoretical) , which is based on scientific and engineering fundamentals , such as material balance, thermodynamics, kinetics , heat , mass and momentum transfer, etc. Rational process analysis is the superior of all. It can provide us most rigorous quantitative co-relations of complex phenomenon.

4. Dynamic vs. Static models: A dynamic model includes time in the model A static model can be defined without involving time

5 Continuous-time vs. Discrete-time dynamic models: Continuous-time models may evolve their variable values continuously during a time period. Discrete-time variables change values a finite number of times during a time period

Stochastic model vs deterministic model:

A deterministic model is one in which every set of variable states is uniquely determined by parameters in the model and by sets of previous states of these variables; therefore, a deterministic model always performs the same way for a given set of initial conditions. Conversely, in a stochastic model—usually called a "statistical model"—randomness is present, and variable states are not described by unique values, but rather by probability distributions

7.3 Simulation

A simulation of a system is the executing the model of the system on a digital computer, and analyzing the execution output. The model can be reconfigured and experimented. The operation of the model can be studied, and hence, properties concerning the behavior of the actual system or its subsystem can be inferred. In its broadest sense, simulation is a tool to evaluate the performance of a system, existing or proposed, under different configurations of interest and over long periods of real time. Children understand the world around them by simulating (with toys and figurines) most of their interactions with other people, animals and objects. As adults, we lose some of this childlike behavior but recapture it later on through computer simulation. Thus **simulation is the employment of computational processes to implement a model representation of the essential features of the behavior of a system**

7.4   Benefits of Modelling and Simulation

1. Using simulations is generally cheaper, safer and sometimes more ethical than conducting real-world experiments. For example, supercomputers are sometimes used to simulate the detonation of nuclear devices and their effects in order to support better preparedness in the event of a nuclear explosion. Similar efforts are conducted to simulate hurricanes and other natural catastrophes.

2. Simulations can often be even more realistic than traditional experiments, as they allow the free configuration of environment parameters found in the operational application field of the final product.

3. Simulations can often be conducted faster than real time. This allows using them for efficient if-then-else analyses of different alternatives, in particular when the necessary data to initialize the simulation can easily be obtained from operational data. This use of simulation adds decision support simulation systems to the tool box of traditional decision support systems.

7.5 Applications of Modeling and Simulation

Modelling and Simulation can be applied to the following areas – Military applications, training & support, designing semiconductors, telecommunications, engineering designs and E-business models.

Additionally, it is used to study the internal structure of a complex system such as the biological system. It is used while optimizing the system design such as routing algorithm, assembly line, etc. It is used to test new designs and policies. It is used to verify analytic solutions.

7.6 Classification of Models

A system can be classified into the following categories.

•   **Discrete-Event Simulation Model** – In this model, the state variable values change only at some discrete points in time where the events occur. Events will only occur at the defined activity time and delays.

- **Stochastic vs. Deterministic Systems** – Stochastic systems are not affected by randomness and their output is not a random variable, whereas deterministic systems are affected by randomness and their output is a random variable.

- **Static vs. Dynamic Simulation** – Static simulation include models which are not affected with time. For example: Monte Carlo Model. Dynamic Simulation include models which are affected with time.

- **Discrete vs. Continuous Systems** – Discrete system is affected by the state variable changes at a discrete point of time. Its behavior is depicted in the following graphical representation.

7.7 Steps in modeling and simulation

Step 1. Identify the problem.

Step 2. Formulate the problem.

Step 3. Collect and process real system data.

Step 4. Formulate and develop a model.

Step 5. Validate the model.

Step 6. Document model for future use.

Step 7. Select appropriate experimental design.

Step 8. Establish experimental conditions for runs.

Step 9. Perform simulation runs.

Step 10. Interpret and present results.

7.8 Examples of Modeling

Curve Fitting - Models to Data

```python
from scipy.optimize import curve_fit
import matplotlib.pyplot as plt

x=[0,1,2,3,4,5]

y=[15,10,9,6,2,0]

def linear_model (x,a,b) :

    return a * x + b

popt, pcov= curve_fit (linear_model, x , y)
print (popt)
# [-2.91428571 14.28571429]

plt.plot(x,y)

plt.show()
```

Polynomial Model

```
import numpy as np
import matplotlib.pyplot as plt

x=[0,1,2,3,4,5]

y=[15,10,9,6,2,0]

plt.plot(x,y,'ok')

model_order=3
p=np.polyfit (x,y,model_order)
print(p)

xstart=-1
xstop=6
increament=0.1

xmodel=np.arange(xstart,xstop, increament)

ymodel= np.polyval( p, xmodel)

plt.plot(xmodel,ymodel, 'r')

# Results [-0.06481481  0.53968254 -4.07010582 14.65873016]
```

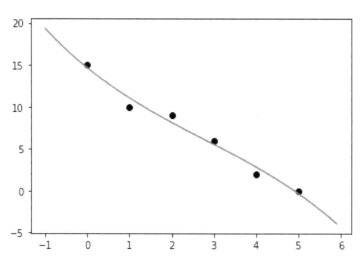

The details of modeling and simulation for real engineering problems are discussed in the subsequent chapters.

Chapter 8

Python for Science and Engineering

8.1 Solving Linear Equations

for linear equations AX=B

where

$$A = \begin{bmatrix} a_{11} & a_{12} & \cdots & a_{1m} \\ a_{21} & a_{22} & \cdot\cdot & a_{2m} \\ \cdots & \cdots & \cdots & \cdots \\ a_{n1} & a_{n2} & \cdots & a_{nm} \end{bmatrix}$$

$$B = \begin{bmatrix} b_{11} \\ b_{21} \\ \cdots \\ b_{n1} \end{bmatrix}$$

$X = A^{-1}B \qquad X = Ainv.B$

```
import numpy as np

A = np.array([[1, 2],
              [3, 4]])

b = np.array([[5],
              [6]])

x = np.linalg.solve(A, b)
print(x)
```

The results come out -4, 4.5

$X_1 - 2x_2 - 3x_3 = 5$

$3X_1 - 4x_2 + 5x_3 = 6$

$7X_1 + 8x_2 + 9x_3 = 9$

```
import numpy as np

import numpy.linalg as la

A = np.array ( [[1,-2,-3 ], [3,-4,5 ],[ 7,8,9 ] ] )

B=np.array ([[5],[6],[9]])

Ainv=la.inv(A)

x=Ainv.dot(B)

print(x)
```

Answer

[[2.47580645], [-0.37903226], [-0.58870968]]

8.2 Interpolation

```
import numpy as np
import matplotlib.pyplot as plt

x = [1, 2, 3]
y = [3, 2, 0]

x_new = 2.5

y_new = np.interp(2.5, x, y)

print("New Interpolated Value:")
print(y_new)

plt.plot(x,y,'o-')
plt.show()
```

8.2.1 Interpolation Example using numpy

import numpy as np

import matplotlib.pyplot as plt

```
x=[1,2,3]
y=[3,2,0]
x_new=2.5
y_new=np.interp(2.5,x,y)
print ("Interpolated value of y=")
print (y_new)
# Interpolated value of y= 1.0
plt.plot (x , y)
output y=1.0
```

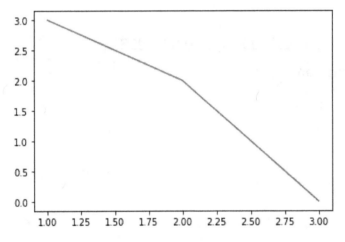

8.2.2 Interpolation Example using scipy.interpolate

```python
import numpy as np
import matplotlib.pyplot as plt
from scipy import interpolate

x = np.arange(0, 10)
y = np.exp(-x/3.0)
f = interpolate.interp1d(x, y)

xnew = np.arange(0, 9, 0.1)
ynew = f(xnew)    # use interpolation function

plt.plot(x, y, 'o', xnew, ynew, '-')
plt.show()
```

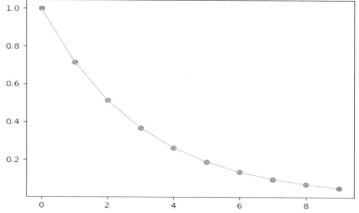

Append

Meaning read data from that row or column of an excel file

E.append(row[0])

I.append(int(row[1]))

8.2.3 Interpolation Example Scipy

```
import numpy as np
import matplotlib.pyplot as plt
from scipy.interpolate import interp1d

x = np.linspace(0, 10, num=11, endpoint=True)
y = np.cos(-x**2/9.0)

f = interp1d(x, y) #linear is default
f2 = interp1d(x, y, kind='cubic')


xnew = np.linspace(0, 10, num=41, endpoint=True)

plt.plot(x, y, 'o', xnew, f(xnew), '-', xnew, f2(xnew), '--')
plt.legend(['data', 'linear', 'cubic'], loc='best')
plt.show()
```

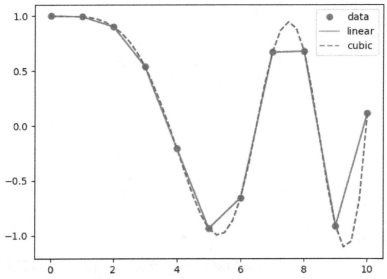

8.3 Curve fitting Model higher order

We have already discussed curve fitting model for linear model in the chapter 3. We will now investigate models of 2nd order, 3rd order, 4th order and 5th order.

We start with a 2nd order model:

$y(x) = ax^2 + bx^2 + c$

```python
import numpy as np
from scipy.optimize import curve_fit
import matplotlib.pyplot as plt

x = [0, 1, 2, 3, 4, 5]
y = [15, 10, 9, 6, 2, 0]


def linear_model(x, a, b, c):
    return a * x**2 + b * x + c

popt, pcov = curve_fit(linear_model, x, y)

print(popt)

plt.plot(x,y, 'ok')


xstart = -1
xstop = 6
increment = 0.1
xmodel = np.arange(xstart, xstop, increment)

a = popt[0]
b = popt[1]
c = popt[2]

ymodel = a *xmodel**2 + b * xmodel + c

plt.plot(xmodel, ymodel, 'b')
```

The Python code gives the following results: the coefficients a, b and c in the model

[0.05357143 -3.18214286 14.46428571]

Here is the Python code for a 5.order model (based on that you can easily create code for 3.order and 4.order models):

```python
import numpy as np
from scipy.optimize import curve_fit
import matplotlib.pyplot as plt

x = [0, 1, 2, 3, 4, 5]
y = [15, 10, 9, 6, 2, 0]

def linear_model(x, a, b, c, d, e, f):
    return a * x**5 + b * x**4 + c * x**3 + d * x**2 + e * x + f

popt, pcov = curve_fit(linear_model, x, y)

print(popt)

plt.plot(x,y, 'ok')

xstart = -1
xstop = 6
increment = 0.1
xmodel = np.arange(xstart,xstop,increment)

a = popt[0]
b = popt[1]
c = popt[2]
d = popt[3]
e = popt[4]
f = popt[5]

ymodel = a * xmodel**5 + b * xmodel**4 + c * xmodel**3 + d * xmodel**2 + e * xmodel + f

plt.plot(xmodel,ymodel, 'm')
```

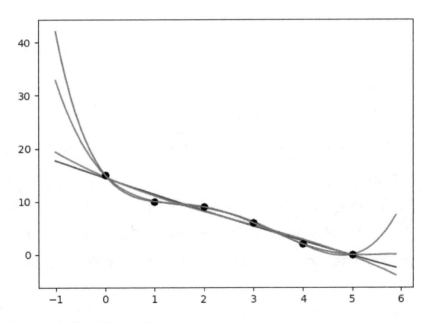

Interpolation Example

8.4 Polynomial Regression using polyfit and polyval functions

We start with a 3rd order model:

$y(x) = ax^3 + bx^2 + cx + d$

```
import numpy as np
import matplotlib.pyplot as plt

# Original Data
x = [0, 1, 2, 3, 4, 5]
y = [15, 10, 9, 6, 2, 0]

plt.plot(x,y, 'ok')


# Finding the Model
model_order = 3

p = np.polyfit(x, y, model_order)
print(p)

# Plot the Model
xstart = -1
xstop = 6
increment = 0.1
xmodel = np.arange(xstart,xstop,increment)

ymodel = np.polyval(p, xmodel)

plt.plot(xmodel,ymodel, 'r')
```

We get the following results:

[-0.06481481 0.53968254 -4.07010582 14.65873016]

This means the following 3rd order model:

$y(x) = -0{:}06x^3 + 0{:}54x^2 - 4.1x + 14.7$

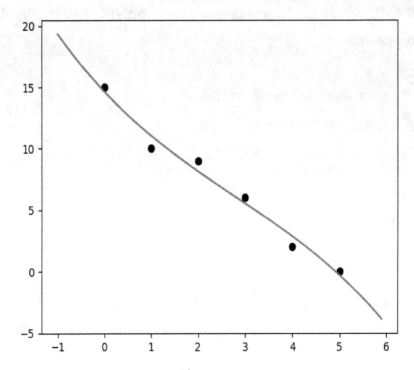

Interpolation Example – 3rd order model

8.5 Least Square Method

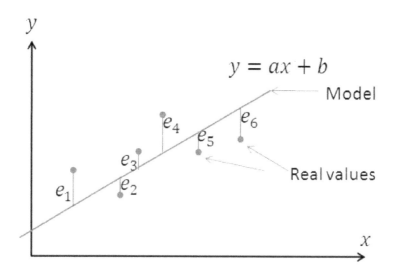

Least Squares Regression in Python

```python
import numpy as np
from scipy import optimize
import matplotlib.pyplot as plt

plt.style.use('seaborn-poster')

# generate x and y
x = np.linspace(0, 1, 101)
y = 1 + x + x * np.random.random(len(x))

# assemble matrix A
A = np.vstack([x, np.ones(len(x))]).T

# turn y into a column vector
y = y[:, np.newaxis]

# Direct least square regression
alpha = np.dot((np.dot(np.linalg.inv(np.dot(A.T,A)),A.T)),y)
print(alpha)
```

Results [[1.459573] [1.02952189]]

```
# plot the results
plt.figure(figsize = (10,8))
plt.plot(x, y, 'b.')
plt.plot(x, alpha[0]*x + alpha[1], 'r')
plt.xlabel('x')
plt.ylabel('y')
plt.show()
```

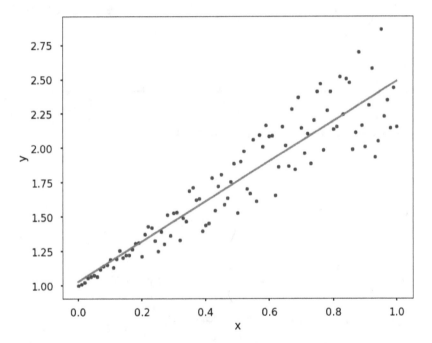

In Python, there are many different ways to conduct the least square regression. For example, we can use packages as NUMPY, SCIPY, STATSMODELS, SKLEARN and so on to get a least square solution

Use numpy.linalg.lstsq

```
alpha = np.linalg.lstsq(A, y, rcond=None)[0]
print(alpha)
```

Results [[1.459573] [1.02952189]]

Use optimize.curve_fit from scipy

```
# generate x and y
x = np.linspace(0, 1, 101)
y = 1 + x + x * np.random.random(len(x))


def func(x, a, b):
    y = a*x + b
    return y


alpha = optimize.curve_fit(func, xdata = x, ydata = y)[0]
print(alpha)
```

8.6 Numerical Differentiation

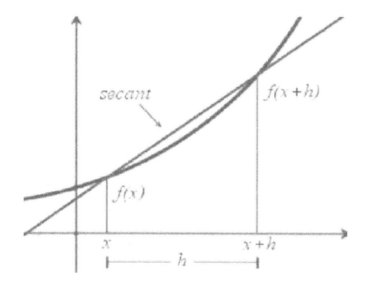

```python
import numpy as np
import matplotlib.pyplot as plt

xstart = -2
xstop = 2.1
increment = 0.1
x = np.arange(xstart, xstop, increment)

y = x**2

plt.plot(x, y)


xstart = -2
xstop = 3
increment = 1
x = np.arange(xstart, xstop, increment)

y = x**2;

plt.plot(x, y, '-o')
```

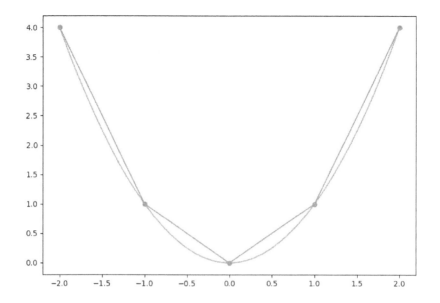

8.7 Numerical Integration

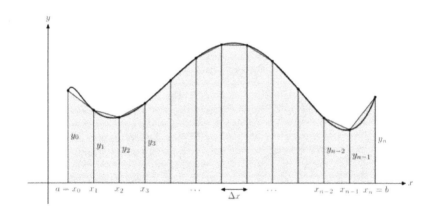

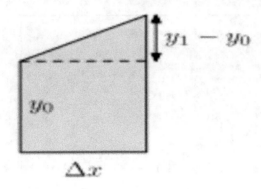

Python Code Trapezoid Rule

```python
import numpy as np
import matplotlib.pyplot as plt

a = 0
b = 1
N = 10

x = np.linspace(a,b,N+1)

y = x**2;

y_right = y[1:]
y_left = y[:-1]


# Trapezoid Rule
dx = (b - a)/N
A = (dx/2) * np.sum(y_right + y_left)

print(A)

plt.plot(x,y)
plt.xlim([0,1]); plt.ylim([0,1]);
```

We get the following results: A = 0.3350

Integration using the module scipy

```
from scipy import integrate

a = 0
b = 1

def y(x):
    return x**2

I = integrate.quad(y, a, b)

print(I)
```

We get the following results:

I = (0.33333333333333337, 3.700743415417189e-15)

Using trapz function of NumPy module

```
import numpy as np

a = 0
b = 1
N = 10
dx = (b - a)/N

x = np.linspace(a,b,N+1)

y = x**2;

I = np.trapz(y,x,dx)

print(I)
```

We get the following results: I = 0.3349

TRY IT! Use numpy.linalg.solve to solve the following equations.

$$4x_1 + 3x_2 - 5x_3 = 2$$
$$-2x_1 - 4x_2 + 5x_3 = 5$$
$$8x_1 + 8x_2 = -3$$

```python
import numpy as np

A = np.array([[4, 3, -5],
              [-2, -4, 5],
              [8, 8, 0]])
y = np.array([2, 5, -3])

x = np.linalg.solve(A, y)
print(x)
```

```
[ 2.20833333 -2.58333333 -0.183333
```

Chapter 9
Image Processing by Python

9.1 Image Processing

Image processing in Python

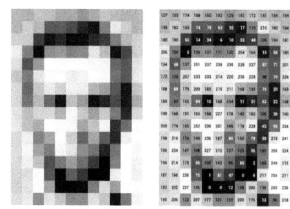 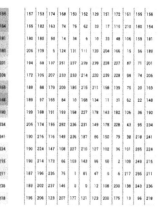

9.2 Image pixel values:

We can think of an image as a set of small samples. These samples are called pixels. For a better understanding, try zoom in on an image as much as possible. We can see the same divided into different squares. These are the pixels and when they are combined together they form an image.

One of the simple ways to represent an image is, in the form of a matrix. We can even create an image using a matrix and save it

On the left, is an image of Lincoln, in the middle, the pixel values are labeled with numbers from 0 to 255, denoting their intensity or brightness and on the right, the numbers in matrix form themselves. Each value in the matrix corresponds to a pixel, which is the smallest element of information present in an image. Check out the image pixel values by just printing the variable that you loaded the image!

print(img)

9.3 Image Resolution

Image resolution could be defined as the number of pixels present in an image. The quality of the image increases when the number of pixels increases. We have seen earlier, the shape of the image which gives the number of rows and columns. This could be said as the resolution of that image. Some of the standard resolutions are that almost everyone knows are 320 x 240 pixels (mostly suitable on small screen devices), 1024 x 768 pixels (appropriate to view on standard computer monitors), 720 x 576 pixels(good to view on standard definition TV sets having 4:3 aspect ratio), 1280 x 720 pixels (for viewing on widescreen monitors),1280 x 1024 pixels (good for viewing on the full-screen size on LCD monitors with 5:4 aspect ratio), 1920 x 1080 pixels (for viewing on HD tv's) and now we even have 4K, 5K, and 8K resolutions which are 3840 x 2160 pixels, 5120 × 2880 pixels and 7,680 x 4,320 pixels respectively supported by ultra high definition monitors and televisions.

When we multiply the number of columns and number of rows, we can obtain the total number of pixels present in the image. For example, in a 320 x 240 image, the total number of pixels present in it is 76,800 pixels.

9.4 Image Processing Frankfurt

Program image_processing.py

```python
import numpy as np
import matplotlib.pyplot as plt
img = plt.imread('frankfurt.png')
print(img[:3])
plt.axis("off")
imgplot = plt.imshow(img)
lum_img = img[:,:,1]
print(lum_img)
[[1. 1. 1. 0.]
 [1. 1. 1. 0.]
 [1. 1. 1. 0.]
 [1. 1. 1. 0.]
 [1. 1. 1. 0.]
 [1. 1. 1. 0.]]
```

```
[[1. 1. 1. 0.]
 [1. 1. 1. 0.]
 [1. 1. 1. 0.]
 ...
 [1. 1. 1. 0.]
 [1. 1. 1. 0.]
 [1. 1. 1. 0.]]
[[1. 1. 1. 0.]
 [1. 1. 1. 0.]
 [1. 1. 1. 0.]
 ...
 [1. 1. 1. 0.]
 [1. 1. 1. 0.]
 [1. 1. 1. 0.]]]
[[1. 1. 1. ... 1. 1. 1.]
 [1. 1. 1. ... 1. 1. 1.]
 [1. 1. 1. ... 1. 1. 1.]
 ...
 [1. 1. 1. ... 1. 1. 1.]
 [1. 1. 1. ... 1. 1. 1.]
 [1. 1. 1. ... 1. 1. 1.]]
```

9.5 Image Processing Charlie Chaplin

Program image_processing2.py

```
import numpy as np
import matplotlib.pyplot as plt
charlie = plt.imread('Chaplin.png')
plt.gray()
print(charlie)
plt.imshow(charlie)
```

```
[[[1. 1. 1. 0.]
  [1. 1. 1. 0.]
  [1. 1. 1. 0.]
  ...
  [1. 1. 1. 0.]
  [1. 1. 1. 0.]
  [1. 1. 1. 0.]]
```

```
[[1. 1. 1. 0.]
 [1. 1. 1. 0.]
 [1. 1. 1. 0.]
 ...
 [1. 1. 1. 0.]
 [1. 1. 1. 0.]
 [1. 1. 1. 0.]]

[[1. 1. 1. 0.]
 [1. 1. 1. 0.]
 [1. 1. 1. 0.]
 ...
 [1. 1. 1. 0.]
 [1. 1. 1. 0.]
 [1. 1. 1. 0.]]

...

[[1. 1. 1. 0.]
 [1. 1. 1. 0.]
 [1. 1. 1. 0.]
 ...
 [1. 1. 1. 0.]
 [1. 1. 1. 0.]
 [1. 1. 1. 0.]]
```

```
[[1. 1. 1. 0.]
 [1. 1. 1. 0.]
 [1. 1. 1. 0.]
 ...
 [1. 1. 1. 0.]
 [1. 1. 1. 0.]
 [1. 1. 1. 0.]]

[[1. 1. 1. 0.]
 [1. 1. 1. 0.]
 [1. 1. 1. 0.]
 ...
 [1. 1. 1. 0.]
 [1. 1. 1. 0.]
 [1. 1. 1. 0.]]]
```

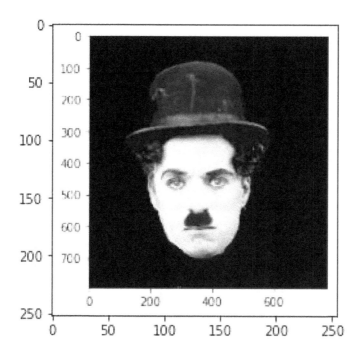

9.6 Image Processing Empire State

Program image_processing3.py

```
from PIL import Image
import numpy as np
import matplotlib.pyplot as pl
# read image to array
im = np.array(Image.open('empire.jpg'))
print("Shape is: {0} of type {1}".format(im.shape, im.dtype))

# read grayscale version to float array
```

```python
im = np.array(Image.open('empire.jpg').convert('L'),'f')
print("Shape is: {0} of type {1}".format(im.shape, im.dtype))

# visualize the pixel value of a small region
col_1, col_2 = 190, 225
row_1, row_2 = 230, 265

# crop using array slicing
crop = im[col_1:col_2,row_1:row_2]
cols, rows = crop.shape

print("Created crop of shape: {0}".format(crop.shape))

# generate all the plots
pl.figure()
pl.imshow(im)
pl.gray()
pl.plot([row_1, row_2, row_2, row_1, row_1], [col_1, col_1,
col_2, col_2, col_1], linewidth=2)
pl.axis('off')

pl.figure()
pl.imshow(crop)
pl.gray()
pl.axis('off')
```

```python
pl.figure()
pl.imshow(crop)
pl.gray()
pl.plot(20*np.ones(cols), linewidth=2)
pl.axis('off')

pl.figure()
pl.plot(crop[20,:])
pl.ylabel("Graylevel value")

from mpl_toolkits.mplot3d import axes3d
fig = pl.figure()
ax = fig.gca(projection='3d')
# surface plot with transparency 0.5
X,Y = np.meshgrid(np.arange(cols),-np.arange(rows))
ax.plot_surface(X, Y, crop, alpha=0.5, cstride=2, rstride=2)

pl.show()
```

Output
Shape is: (800, 569, 3) of type uint8
Shape is: (800, 569) of type float32
Created crop of shape: (35, 35)

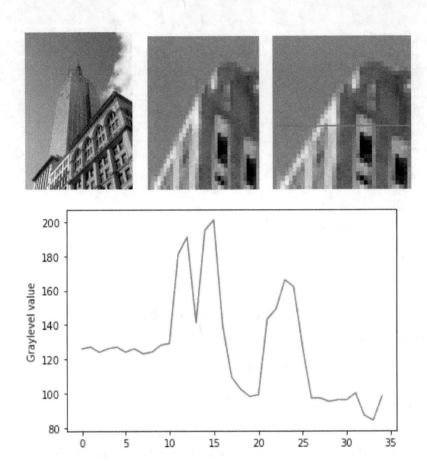

9.7 MNIST Dataset

The MNIST dataset consists of images of digits from a variety of scanned documents. Each image is a 28X28 pixel square. In this dataset 60,000 images are used to train the model and 10,000 images are used to test the model. There are 10 digits (0 to 9) or 10 classes to predict.

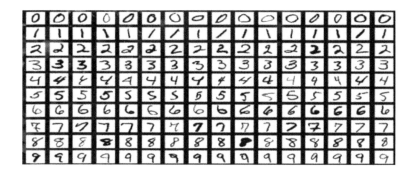

9.7.1 Loading the MNIST Dataset

Install the TensorFlow library and import the dataset as a train and test dataset.

Plot the sample output of the image

!pip install tensorflow

from keras.datasets import mnist

import matplotlib.pyplot as plt

(X_train,y_train), (X_test, y_test)= mnist.load_data()

plt.subplot()

plt.imshow(X_train[9], cmap=plt.get_cmap('gray'))

P9.7.2 Program image_processing4.py

import numpy as np

import pandas as pd

import matplotlib.pyplot as plt #these are required to take the image as input and output

import cv2 # this library is required to use openCv

img = cv2.imread("Chaplin.png")

Here 'img' is the variable storing the image, and 'Input_image' is the image taken from the directory.

print(img) # by printing the we img we get a 2-D array as discused.

```
[[[255 255 255]
  [255 255 255]
  [255 255 255]

  ...

  [255 255 255]
  [255 255 255]
  [255 255 255]]

 [[255 255 255]
  [255 255 255]
  [255 255 255]

  ...

  [255 255 255]
  [255 255 255]
  [255 255 255]]

 [[255 255 255]
  [255 255 255]
  [255 255 255]

  ...

  [255 255 255]
```

```
  [255 255 255]
  [255 255 255]]


...

[[255 255 255]
 [255 255 255]
 [255 255 255]
 ...
 [255 255 255]
 [255 255 255]
 [255 255 255]]

[[255 255 255]
 [255 255 255]
 [255 255 255]
 ...
 [255 255 255]
 [255 255 255]
 [255 255 255]]

[[255 255 255]
 [255 255 255]
 [255 255 255]
 ...
 [255 255 255]
```

[255 255 255]

[255 255 255]]]

Digital Image processing features a wide selection of applications in the world. In almost every technical aspect we use digital image processing.

- In Medical life, Image processing has a very wide range of applications like Diagnosing a disease using X-ray, Thermography, Mammography, Size of the tumor present inside the body, etc.

- Removing noise, background, and Image restoration and sharpening.

- Video processing and live telecasting.

- Pattern recognition

- Image Transmission and Image Encoding

Chapter 10
Artificial Intelligence (AI)

10.1 Basic Concept of AI

Let us try to understand what is the basic difference between a Computer and a human. A computer can do multiple operations of mathematics, writing texts etc hundreds times faster than a very intelligent human. A computer can memorizes and save text , data etc of huge amount which our brain cannot.

We also forget but computer do not forget. Can computer give logic of any event to understand better, learn more and become scholar and wise. Answer is big NO. A human brain can compare one object with another, one incident with another, one man with another and learn by itself through logics since childhood as he or she grows.

That is why human being is called most intelligent animal on earth. With decreasing intelligent human population particularly in the developed countries like Japan , Germany,

United States, etc, the need of the hour to survive is to innovate intelligent machines which can think like like us by programming and building software to computers and make them ARTIFICIAL INTELLIGENCE (AI).

If human being was not there, AI would not have existed, AI is serving the lazy society who believes on fast result rather than rigorous failures to get a result.

AI is done by statistical modeling and simulation with huge number of data which is also called data science.

Let us try to understand it, through illustration of an example, in fig

10.2 Architecture of AI

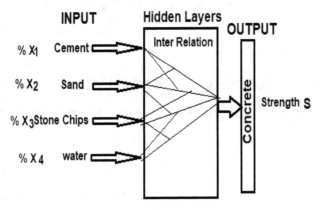

$$S = w1.x1 + w2.x2 + w3.x3 + w4.x4$$

Fig Understanding AI with an example of producing best Cement concrete pillar

10.3 Input and Output AI

Variation of proportionate of input like cement, sand , stone and water will produce different strength of concrete. Generate a lot of sets of input data and output data. Train the computer with input set and output like for instance if the stone % is high , strength is high or if sand is high, strength is low. This way computer ill understand like human, ok if this is more, that is less. Similar to how we learned cooking if sugar is more its taste is more sweetie or if this spice is more the taste will be like this.

Now we take a test of the computer whether it can predict with a new set of unknown input. Suppose we see it can predict sand proportion to strength correctly but not stone chips, then we increase the value weight w3 (weight for stone) and decrease w1 (weight for cement) , to make it learn more on stone proportion to strength and may be devote somewhat less learning for sand , which the computer has already learned.

10.4 AI Machine Learning

This way through a number of loops , a time will come when the computer will be able predict results for any sets of known input to over 90% correct prediction of output. So this way Artificial Intelligence (AI) is taught to the machine through machine learning.

AI is carried out with **NEURAL NETWORK**, which has been discussed in detail in the next chapter 9 with python coding

10.5 Application of AI

Some examples of application of AI are given below

Intelligence	Description	Example
Linguistic intelligence	The ability to speak, recognize, and use mechanisms of phonology (speech sounds), syntax (grammar), and semantics (meaning).	Narrators, Orators
Musical intelligence	The ability to create, communicate with, and understand meanings made of sound, understanding of pitch, rhythm.	Musicians, Singers, Composers
Logical-mathematical intelligence	The ability to use and understand relationships in the absence of action or objects. It is also the ability to understand complex and abstract ideas.	Mathematicians, Scientists
Spatial intelligence	The ability to perceive visual or spatial information, change it, and re-create visual images without reference to the objects, construct 3D	Map readers, Astronauts, Physicists

10.6 AI Composition

It is composed of −

Reasoning

Learning

Problem Solving

Perception

Linguistic Intelligence

10.6.1 Reasoning

It is the set of processes that enable us to provide basis for judgment, making decisions, and prediction. There are broadly two types –

Inductive Reasoning	Deductive Reasoning
It conducts specific observations to makes broad general statements	If something is true of a class of things in general, it is also true for all members of that class.
Example – "Nita is a teacher. Nita is studious. Therefore, All teachers are studious."	Example – "All women of age above 60 years are grandmothers. Shalini is 65 years. Therefore, Shalini is a grandmother."

10.6.2 Learning

It is learning by listening and hearing. For example, students listening to recorded audio

by remembering sequences of events that one has witnessed or experienced

by watching and imitating others. For example, child tries to learn by mimicking her parent.

10.6.3 Problem Solving

It is the process in which one perceives and tries to arrive at a desired solution from a present situation by taking some path, which is blocked by known or unknown hurdles.

Problem solving also includes **decision making**, which is the process of selecting the best suitable alternative out of multiple alternatives to reach the desired goal.

10.6.4 Perception

Perception presumes **sensing**. In humans, perception is aided by sensory organs. In the domain of AI, perception mechanism puts the data acquired by the sensors together in a meaningful manner

10.6.5 Linguistic Intelligence

It is one's ability to use, comprehend, speak, and write the verbal and written language. It is important in interpersonal communication.

10.6.5 Machine Learning

It is one of the most popular fields of AI. The basic concept of this filed is to make the machine learning from data as the human beings can learn from his/her experience. It contains learning models on the basis of which the predictions can be made on unknown data.

10.6.6 Logic

It is another important field of study in which mathematical logic is used to execute the computer programs. It contains rules and facts to perform pattern matching, semantic analysis, etc.

10.6.7 Searching

This field of study is basically used in games like chess, tic-tac-toe. Search algorithms give the optimal solution after searching the whole search space.

10.7 Artificial neural networks

This is a network of efficient computing systems the central theme of which is borrowed from the analogy of biological neural networks. ANN can be used in robotics, speech recognition, speech processing, etc.

10.8 Genetic Algorithm

Genetic algorithms help in solving problems with the assistance of more than one program. The result would be based on selecting the fittest.

10.9 Application of AI

10.9.1 Gaming

AI plays crucial role in strategic games such as chess, poker, tic-tac-toe, etc., where machine can think of large number of possible positions based on heuristic knowledge.

10.9.2 Natural Language Processing

It is possible to interact with the computer that understands natural language spoken by humans.

Expert Systems

There are some applications which integrate machine, software, and special information to impart reasoning and advising. They provide explanation and advice to the users.

Vision Systems

These systems understand, interpret, and comprehend visual input on the computer. For example,

☐ A spying airplane takes photographs, which are used to figure out spatial information or map of the areas.

☐ Doctors use clinical expert system to diagnose the patient.

☐ Police use computer software that can recognize the face of criminal with the stored portrait made by forensic artist.

10.9.3 Speech Recognition

Some intelligent systems are capable of hearing and comprehending the language in terms of sentences and their meanings while a human talks to it. It can handle different accents, slang words, noise in the background, change in human's noise due to cold, etc.

10.9.4 Handwriting Recognition

The handwriting recognition software reads the text written on paper by a pen or on screen by a stylus. It can recognize the shapes of the letters and convert it into editable text.

10.9.5 Intelligent Robots

Robots are able to perform the tasks given by a human. They have sensors to detect physical data from the real world such as light, heat, temperature, movement, sound, bump, and pressure. They have efficient processors, multiple sensors and huge memory, to exhibit intelligence. In addition, they are capable of learning from their mistakes and they can adapt to the new environment.

10.10 Simulating Human Thinking

Cognitive modeling is basically the field of study within computer science that deals with the study and simulating the thinking process of human beings. The main task of AI is to make machine think like human. The most important feature of human thinking process is problem solving. That is why more or less cognitive modeling tries to understand how humans can solve the problems. After that this model can be used for various AI applications such as machine learning, robotics, natural language processing, etc. Following is the diagram of different thinking levels of human brain:

Chapter 11
Neural Network

11.1 Introduction

An artificial neural network (ANN) is a non linear statistical data modeling operating system that can be used to model complex relationship between input and output variables, through training, using huge number of experimentally generated data. NNs are capable of generalizing experience obtained in the course of learning. As a result, it becomes possible to simulate the situations, which are absent in the set of experimental results. Fig 11.1 illustrates how output is computed from sets of input.

11.2 Architecture

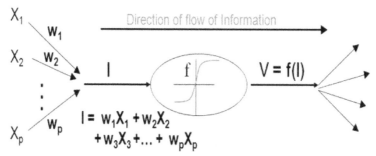

$$I = w_1X_1 + w_2X_2 + w_3X_3 + \ldots + w_pX_p$$

$$V = f(I)$$

Fig 6.1 Schematically shows the relationship between Input and output in ANN through transfer function

11.3 Method

The steps in Artificial neural network (ANN) as follows.

ANN

•   Receives Inputs X_1 X_2 ...X_p from experimental data or real data

•   Inputs fed-in through connections with 'weights'

•   Total Input = Weighted sum of inputs from all sources

•   Transfer function (Activation function) converts the input to output

•   Output goes to other neurons or environment

There can be three types of transfer function as shown in fig6.2. The ANN consists of (i) architecture of the neural network, (ii) training algorithm, and (iii) transfer function. The term "architecture of the neural network" refers to the number of the layers in the NN , that is input, hidden and output layers and as shown in fig 6.3.. The numbers of neurons in the input layer and the output layer are determined by the numbers of input and output parameters, respectively. In order to find the optimal architecture, different numbers of neurons in the hidden layer are attempted (fig 6.3). At the input layer, each of neutrons has certain informative inputs which are equal to the number of independent input parameters of the system, and a certain number of outputs. The output parameter is calculated by substituting a set of input parameters into a certain function (choice of transfer function fig2) taking into account the corresponding set of weight coefficients. In order to find the optimal architecture, different numbers of neurons in the hidden layer are attempted.

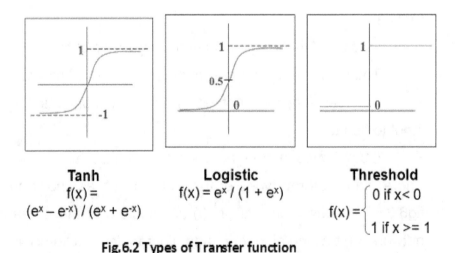

Tanh	Logistic	Threshold
$f(x) =$ $(e^x - e^{-x}) / (e^x + e^{-x})$	$f(x) = e^x / (1 + e^x)$	$f(x) = \begin{cases} 0 \text{ if } x < 0 \\ 1 \text{ if } x >= 1 \end{cases}$

Fig.6.2 Types of Transfer function

11.3.1 Training

ANN needs training to operate and is capable of generalizing experience obtained in the course of learning. Usually, neural networks are trained using a large number of input with corresponding output data (input/output pairs) so that a particular set of inputs produces, as nearly as possible, a specific set of target outputs, by adjusting the weight associated with each connection (synapse) between neurons. As a result, it becomes possible to predict the situations, which are absent in the set of experimental results.

Given the Architecture There are weights to decide.
$$\underline{W} = (W_1, W_2, ..., W_8)$$
Training Data: $(Y_i, X1_i, X2_i, ..., Xp_i)$ i= 1,2,...,n
Given a particular choice of $\underline{W}$, Y's are predicted as ($V_1, V_2, ..., V_n$)
They are *function* of $\underline{W}$.
$\underline{W}$ is chosen such that over all prediction, the error **E** is minimizedfrom the following eqn.

$$E = \Sigma (Yi - Vi)^2$$

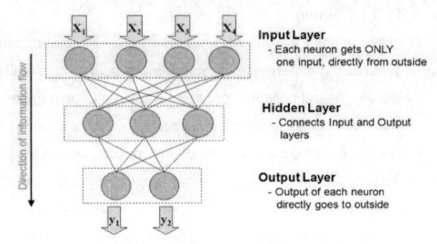

Fig 6.3 Architect of NN , consisting of Input, hidden and Output layer

There are many different training algorithms. The details for the NN training algorithms are given in [9]. In order to achieve the best result, different training algorithms were attempted including Batch Gradient Descent, Batch Gradient Descent with Momentum, One-step-secant, Scaled Conjugate Gradient, Resilient Back propagation, Variable Learning Rate, and Levenberg-Marquardt. Fig 11.4 illustrates feed forward and back propagation method.

The steps are as follows
- Start with a random set of weights.
- Feed forward the first observation through the net

X_1 Network V_1 ; Error = $(Y_1 - V_1)$

- Adjust the weights so that this error is reduced (network fits the first observation well)
- Feed forward the second observation. Adjust weights to fit the second observation well
- Keep repeating till you reach the last observation This finishes one CYCLE through the data
- Perform many such training cycles till the overall prediction error **E** is small.

11.3.2 Back propagation method

In the Back propagation method ,Each weight 'Shares the Blame' for prediction error with other weights. Back Propagation algorithm decides how to distribute the blame among all weights and adjust the weights accordingly. Small portion of blame leads to small adjustment. Large portion of the blame leads to large adjustment. The weight adjustment formula in Back Propagation are as follows

V_i – the prediction for ith observation – is a function of the network weights vector $\underline{W}$ = (W_1, W_2,....)

Hence, E, the total prediction error is also a function of W

$E(\underline{W}) = \Sigma\,[\,Yi - Vi(\underline{W}\,)\,]^2$

11.3.3 Gradient Descent Method :

For every individual weight W_i, updation formula looks like

$W_{new} = W_{old} + \alpha * (\partial E / \partial W)|_{Wold}$, α = Learning Parameter (between 0 and 1)

Another slight variation is also used sometimes

$W_{(t+1)} = W_{(t)} + \alpha * (\partial E / \partial W)|_{w(t)} + \beta * (W_{(t)} - W_{(t-1)})$, β = Momentum (between 0 and 1)

- Plot E vs (w_1, w_2) - a 3-D surface - **'Error Surface'**
- Aim is to identify that pair for which E is minimum
- That means – identify the pair for which the height of the error surface is minimum.

11.3.4 Gradient Descent Algorithm

- Start with a random point (w_1, w_2)
- Move to a 'better' point (w'_1, w'_2) where the height of error surface is lower. Keep moving till you reach (w^*_1, w^*_2), where the error is minimum

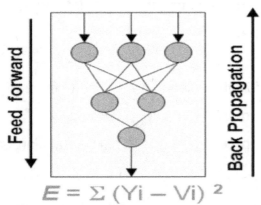

$$E = \Sigma (Yi - Vi)^2$$

Fig.6.4 Feed forward and back propagation method in ANN

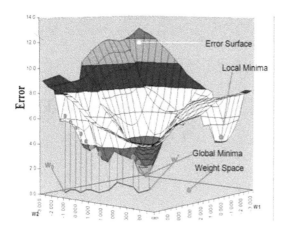

Fig.6.5 Showing Global error minima

11.4 Applications

Neural networks have been successfully applied to broad spectrum of data-intensive applications. The list below is based on real-world success stories.

11.4.1 .Data Mining:

a. Prediction of a property of material ;

b. Response and system Modeling Identification ;

c. Time Series Analysis , dynamic modeling ;

11.4.2 Energy

a.   Energy   Demand   Forecasting

b.   Predicting   Gas/Coal   Index   Prices

c. Power Control Systems

11.4.3 Material Science

a. Material Identification

b. Chemical Systems Analysis

c. Process Optimization

11.4.4   **Finance**   **and**   **Marketing**

a. Stock Market Prediction

b. Price Forecasting

c. Sales Forecasting

11.5 Examples Python Codes

Python Code

11.5.1 simple Neural Network

```python
import network

size = [25, 3, 1]

inputs = [[0, 0, 0, 0, 0, 0, 1, 1, 1, 0, 0, 1, 0, 1, 0, 0, 1, 1, 1, 0,1, 0, 0, 0, 0],
          [0, 1, 0, 0, 0, 0, 1, 1, 1, 0, 0, 1, 0, 1, 0,0, 1, 1, 1, 0, 1, 0, 0, 0, 0],
          [0, 1, 0, 0, 0, 0, 1, 0, 1, 0, 0, 1, 0, 0, 0,0, 0, 1, 1, 0, 1, 0, 0, 0, 0]]

targets = [[1.0], [1.0], [0.0]]

test_inputs = [[0, 0, 0, 1, 0,0, 0, 0, 1, 0,0, 1, 0, 0, 0,0, 0, 1, 1, 0,1, 0, 0, 0, 0],
               [1, 0, 0, 1, 0,0, 1, 1, 1, 0,0, 1, 0, 1, 0,0, 1, 1, 1, 0,1, 0, 0, 0, 0]]


nt = network.Network(size)
# nt.Load_Weights_and_Biases("Data")
nt.Train(epoch=10000, input_data=inputs, target_data=targets,
        batch_size=3, learning_rate=0.1, show_results=True)
print(nt.Feedforward(test_inputs[0]), nt.Feedforward(test_inputs[1]))
```

The input size is of 25 variables and 3 sets of data, '1' means yes it will occur '0' means no it will not occur. Direct is the output. For example say you are cooking chicken curry with 25 types of spices, say turmeric, garlic, onion etc. So you have made 3 chicken curry with 3 different sets of spice addition and the result (targets) '1' means very tasty and '0' means worst .

With the above input and target data , you develop neural network with training , testing and prediction. Take learning rate is 0.1, the no of times the loop will run is 10,000 and you take feedforward technique. After NN has been developed you use it to find out chicken curry taste with unknown spice mixtures given in test_inputs. Here is the result.

[0.06707534714223767] [0.9711465752268091]

That is the second spice mix is excellent , the first is bad

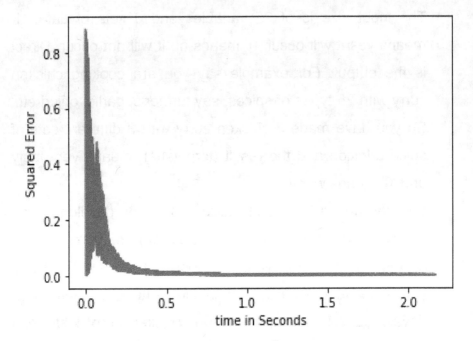

And the fig above shows how the NN prediction error comes down to close to zero in less than a second

11.5.2 Example 2

```
import numpy as np
import matplotlib.pyplot as plt

inputs = np.array([[15, 3, 8],      outputs = np.array([[17.23],
                   [15,2.5,7],                          [21.48],
                   [15,2,7],                            [23.97],
                   [15,1.5,7],                          [25.98],
                   [15,0.8,7], _  .                      [27.5],
                   [17, 0.8,7] ])                       [28.32]])
```

```python
# create NeuralNetwork class
class NeuralNetwork:

    # intialize variables in class
    def __init__(self, inputs, outputs):
        self.inputs  = inputs
        self.outputs = outputs
        # initialize weights as .50 for simplicity
        self.weights = np.array([[.50], [.50], [.50]])
        self.error_history = []
        self.epoch_list = []

#activation function ==> S(x) = 1/1+e^(-x)
def sigmoid(self, x, deriv=False):
    if deriv == True:
        return x * (1 - x)
    return 1 / (1 + np.exp(-x))

# data will flow through the neural network.
def feed_forward(self):
    self.hidden = self.sigmoid(np.dot(self.inputs, self.weights))

# going backwards through the network to update weights
def backpropagation(self):
    self.error  = self.outputs - self.hidden
    delta = self.error * self.sigmoid(self.hidden, deriv=True)
    self.weights += np.dot(self.inputs.T, delta)




# train the neural net for 25,000 iterations
def train(self, epochs=25000):
    for epoch in range(epochs):
        # flow forward and produce an output
        self.feed_forward()
        # go back though the network to make corrections based on the output
        self.backpropagation()
        # keep track of the error history over each epoch
        self.error_history.append(np.average(np.abs(self.error)))
        self.epoch_list.append(epoch)
```

```python
# function to predict output on new and unseen input data
def predict(self, new_input):
    prediction = self.sigmoid(np.dot(new_input, self.weights))
    return prediction
    print(prediction)

    plt.figure(figsize=(15,5))
    plt.plot(outputs, prediction)
    plt.xlabel('outputs')
    plt.ylabel('prediction')
    plt.show()


# create neural network
NN = NeuralNetwork(inputs, outputs)
# train neural network
NN.train()

# create two new examples to predict
example = np.array([[15, 2.8, 8]])
example_2 = np.array([[17, 3.4, 9]])

# print the predictions for both examples
print(NN.predict(example), - Correct: ', example[0][0])
print(NN.predict(example_2) - Correct ', example_2[0][0])

# plot the error over the entire training duration
plt.figure(figsize=(15,5))
plt.plot(NN.epoch_list, NN.error_history)
plt.xlabel('Epoch')
plt.ylabel('Error')
plt.show()
```

Predicted example 1 =19.23, example2 = 22.35

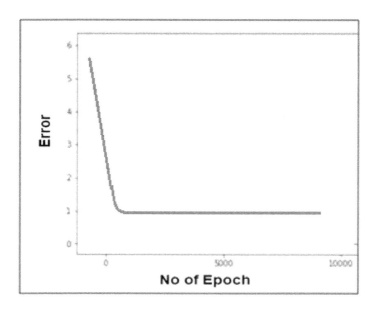

Chapter 12

Python Applications

12.1 Optimization

Optimization typically deals with finding the "best result," or optimum solution, of a problem. Thus, in the context of modeling, they are often termed *prescriptive* models since they can be used to prescribe a course of action or the best design

The optimum is the point where the curve is flat. In mathematical terms, this corresponds to the x value where the derivative $f\_(x)$ is equal to zero. Additionally, the second derivative, $f\_\_(x)$, indicates whether the optimum is a minimum or a maximum: if $f\_\_(x) < 0$, the point is a maximum; if $f\_\_(x) > 0$, the point is a minimum.

12.1.1 Examples of optimization problems in engineering

. Design aircraft for minimum weight and maximum strength.

• Optimal trajectories of space vehicles.

• Design civil engineering structures for minimum cost.

• Design water-resource projects like dams to mitigate flood damage while yielding maximum hydropower.

• Predict structural behavior by minimizing potential energy.

• Material-cutting strategy for minimum cost.

• Design pump and heat transfer equipment for maximum efficiency.

- Maximize power output of electrical networks and machinery while minimizing heat generation.
- Shortest route of salesperson visiting various cities during one sales trip.
- Optimal planning and scheduling.
- Statistical analysis and models with minimum error.
- Optimal pipeline networks.
- Inventory control.
- Maintenance planning to minimize cost.
- Minimize waiting and idling times.
- Design waste treatment systems to meet water-quality standards at least cost.

Example Basic Optimization

$f(x) = x^2 + 2x + 1$

```
from scipy import optimize

xmin = -5
xmax = 5


def y(x):
    return x**2 + 2*x + 1

x_min = optimize.fminbound(y, xmin, xmax)

print(x_min)
```

The result becomes: xmin = -1.0

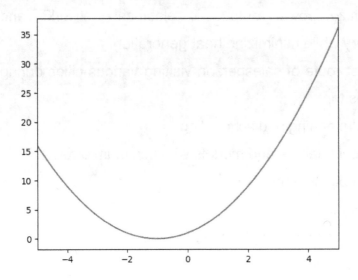

12.2 Linear programming Python

Linear programming (LP) is an optimization approach that deals with meeting a desired objective such as maximizing profit or minimizing cost in the presence of constraints such as limited resources. The term linear connotes that the mathematical functions representing both the objective and the constraints are linear. The term programming does not mean "computer programming," but rather, connotes "scheduling" or "setting an agenda"

The basic linear programming problem consists of two major parts: the objective function and a set of constraints. For a maximization problem, the objective function is generally expressed as

Maximize $Z = c_1x_1 + c_2x_2 + \cdots + c_nx_n$ (4.3)

where c_j = payoff of each unit of the jth activity that is undertaken and x_j = magnitude of the jth activity. Thus, the value of the objective function, Z, is the total payoff due to the total number of activities, n.

The constraints can be represented generally as

$$a_{i1}x_1 + a_{i2}x_2 + \cdots + a_{in}x_n \leq b_i \tag{4.4}$$

where a_{ij} = amount of the ith resource that is consumed for each unit of the jth activity and b_i = amount of the ith resource that is available. That is, the resources are limited. The second general type of constraint specifies that all activities must have a positive value, $x_i \geq 0$

12.2.1 Graphical method

Linear programming optimization can be done by drawing linear lines of the objective function and the constrains and then moving the the straight line of the objective function to the maximum possible value within the area enclosed by the constrains. It has been illustrated by the following example and the graph is shown in

Example

Objective function MAXIMIZE: **Z = 3 X1 + 2 X2**

Constrains

| 2 | X1 | + | 1 | X2 | ≤ | 18 |

| 2 | X1 | + | 3 | X2 | ≤ | 42 |

$3X1 + 1X2 \leq 24$

$X1, X2 \geq 0$

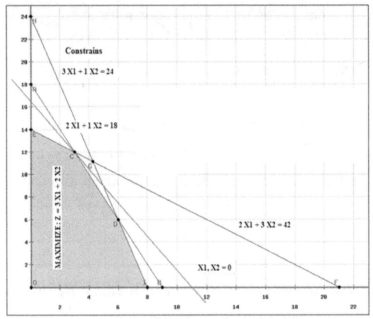

Fig. 4.1 Graphical smethod of Linear programming of maximization

12.2.2 The Simplex Method

The simplex method is predicated on the assumption that the optimal solution will be an extreme point. Thus, the approach must be able to discern whether during problem solution an extreme point occurs. To do this, the constraint equations are reformulated as equalities by introducing what are called slack variables.

Slack Variables :

As the name implies, a *slack variable* measures how much of a constrained resource is available, that is, how much "slack" of the resource is available. Slack variable represents an unused quaintly of resources ; it is added to less than or equal ($\leq$) to type constraints in order to get an equality constraint.

Surplus Variables :

A surplus variable represents the amount by which solution values exceed a resource. These variables are also called 'Negative Slack Variables' . Surplus variables like slack variables carry a zero coefficient in the objective function. it is added to greater than or equal to ($\geq$) type constraints in order to get an equality constraint.

Artificial Variables :

Artificial variables are added to those constraints with equality (=) and greater than or equal to ($\geq$) sign. An Artificial variable is added to the constraints to get an initial solution to an LP problem. Artificial variables have no meaning in a physical sense and are not only used as a tool for generating an initial solution to an LP problem. It is taken as = **-M** for Maximization and **+M** for minimization where M is arbitary large value to force artificial varible out of the solution

A linear programming model has to be extended to comply with the requirements of the simplex procedure , that is,

1. All equations must be equalities.
2. All variables must be present in all equations.

(I) In the case of '≤ ' constraints, slack variables are added to the actual variables to make the equation an equality.

(II) In the case of '≥' constraints, surplus variables are used to make the equation an equality.

Example Linear programming Python

$$
\left\{
\begin{array}{ll}
\min & -4x + 9y - z + 3w \\
\\
\text{s.t.} & 7x - 23y + 5z + 9w \leq 56 \\
& -5x + 3y + z \leq 7 \\
& 4x - 8y + 12z + 4w \geq 1 \\
& 3x + 2y + 9z + 10w \geq 6 \\
& -16x + 28y + 5z + 8w = 5 \\
& -5y + 3z + 2w = 8 \\
& x, y, z, w \geq 0
\end{array}
\right.
$$

```python
from scipy.optimize import linprog
import numpy as np

A_ub = np.array([[7, -23, 5, 9], [-5, 3, 1, 0], [-4, 8, -12, -4], [-3, -2, -9, -10],
    [-1, 0, 0, 0], [0, -1, 0, 0], [0, 0, -1, 0], [0, 0, 0, -1]])
A_eq = np.array([[-16, 28, 5, 8], [0, -5, 3, 2]])
b_ub = np.array([56, 7, -1, -6, 0, 0, 0, 0])
b_eq = np.array([5, 8])
c = np.array([-4, 9, -1, 3])

linprog(c=c, A_ub=A_ub, b_ub=b_ub, A_eq=A_eq, b_eq=b_eq, method="simplex")
```

The result we get is:

con: array([5.68434189e-13, -2.84217094e-14])

fun: -60.305084745761874

message: 'Optimization terminated successfully.'

nit: 9

slack: array([5.68434189e-13,   2.19237288e+02,
7.02389831e+02,

7.75508475e+02,   7.26101695e+01,
3.17457627e+01,

5.55762712e+01, 0.00000000e+00])

status: 0

success: True

x: array([72.61016949, 31.74576271, 55.57627119,

0.   ])

12.3 Chemistry, and Chemical engineering

12.3.1 Parsing formulae

```
from chempy import Substance
ferricyanide = Substance.from_formula('Fe(CN)6-3')
ferricyanide.composition == {0: -3, 26: 1, 6: 6, 7: 6}
True
print(ferricyanide.unicode_name)
```

Fe(CN)$_6^{3-}$

```
 print(ferricyanide.latex_name + ", " + ferricyanide.html_name)
```

Fe(CN)_{6}^{3-}, Fe(CN)₆³⁻

```
 print('%.3f' % ferricyanide.mass)
211.955
```

12.3.2 Balancing stoichiometry of a chemical reaction

```
from chempy import balance_stoichiometry  # Main reaction in NASA's booster rockets:
reac, prod = balance_stoichiometry({'NH4ClO4', 'Al'}, {'Al2O3', 'HCl', 'H2O', 'N2'})
from pprint import pprint
pprint(reac)
{'Al': 10, 'NH4ClO4': 6}
pprint(prod)
{'Al2O3': 5, 'H2O': 9, 'HCl': 6, 'N2': 3}
from chempy import mass_fractions
for fractions in map(mass_fractions, [reac, prod]):
...     pprint({k: '{0:.3g} wt%'.format(v*100) for k, v in fractions.items()})
...
{'Al': '27.7 wt%', 'NH4ClO4': '72.3 wt%'}
{'Al2O3': '52.3 wt%', 'H2O': '16.6 wt%', 'HCl': '22.4 wt%', 'N2': '8.62 wt%'}
```

12.3.3 Chemical equilibria

```python
from chempy import Equilibrium
from chempy.chemistry import Species
water_autop = Equilibrium({'H2O'}, {'H+', 'OH-'}, 10**-14)  # unit "molar" assumed
ammonia_prot = Equilibrium({'NH4+'}, {'NH3', 'H+'}, 10**-9.24)  # same here
from chempy.equilibria import EqSystem
substances = map(Species.from_formula, 'H2O OH- H+ NH3 NH4+'.split())
eqsys = EqSystem([water_autop, ammonia_prot], substances)
print('\n'.join(map(str, eqsys.rxns)))  # "rxns" short for "reactions"
H2O = H+ + OH-; 1e-14
NH4+ = H+ + NH3; 5.75e-10
from collections import defaultdict
init_conc = defaultdict(float, {'H2O': 1, 'NH3': 0.1})
x, sol, sane = eqsys.root(init_conc)
assert sol['success'] and sane
print(sorted(sol.keys()))  # see package "pyneqsys" for more info
['fun', 'intermediate_info', 'internal_x_vecs', 'nfev', 'njev', 'success', 'x', 'x_vecs']
print(', '.join('%.2g' % v for v in x))
1, 0.0013, 7.6e-12, 0.099, 0.0013
```

12.3.4 Chemical kinetics

```python
from chempy import ReactionSystem  # The rate constants below are arbitrary
rsys = ReactionSystem.from_string("""2 Fe+2 + H2O2 -> 2 Fe+3 + 2 OH-; 42
    2 Fe+3 + H2O2 -> 2 Fe+2 + O2 + 2 H+; 17
    H+ + OH- -> H2O; 1e10
    H2O -> H+ + OH-; 1e-4
    Fe+3 + 2 H2O -> FeOOH(s) + 3 H+; 1
    FeOOH(s) + 3 H+ -> Fe+3 + 2 H2O; 2.5""")  # "[H2O]" = 1.0 (actually 55.4 at RT)
from chempy.kinetics.ode import get_odesys
odesys, extra = get_odesys(rsys)
from collections import defaultdict
import numpy as np
tout = sorted(np.concatenate((np.linspace(0, 23), np.logspace(-8, 1))))
c0 = defaultdict(float, {'Fe+2': 0.05, 'H2O2': 0.1, 'H2O': 1.0, 'H+': 1e-7, 'OH-': 1e-7})
result = odesys.integrate(tout, c0, atol=1e-12, rtol=1e-14)
import matplotlib.pyplot as plt
_ = plt.subplot(1, 2, 1)
_ = result.plot(names=[k for k in rsys.substances if k != 'H2O'])
_ = plt.legend(loc='best', prop={'size': 9}); _ = plt.xlabel('Time'); _ =
plt.ylabel('Concentration')
_ = plt.subplot(1, 2, 2)
_ = result.plot(names=[k for k in rsys.substances if k != 'H2O'], xscale='log', yscale='log')
_ = plt.legend(loc='best', prop={'size': 9}); _ = plt.xlabel('Time'); _ =
plt.ylabel('Concentration')
_ = plt.tight_layout()
plt.show()
```

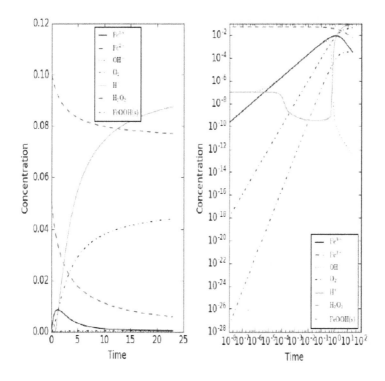

12.4 Student Management System

```python
import os
import platform

global listStd #Making ListStd As Super Global Variable
listStd = ["yugesh", "kishor", "gajen", "Gopi"] #List Of Students

def manageStudent(): #Function For The Student Management System

    x = "#" * 30
    y = "=" * 28
    global bye #Making Bye As Super Global Variable
    bye = "\n {}\n# {} #\n# ===> Brought To You By <===  #\n# ===>
code projects.org <===  #\n# {} #\n {}".format(x, y, y, x)
    #Printing Welcome Message And options For This Program
    print("""


    ----------------------------------------------------------
    |==========================================================| |
    |========= Welcome To Student Management System =========|
    |==========================================================|
    ----------------------------------------------------------


Enter 1 : To View Student's List
Enter 2 : To Add New Student
Enter 3 : To Search Student
Enter 4 : To Remove Student


        """)
```

```python
try: #Using Exceptions For Validation
    userInput = int(input("Please Select An Above Option: ")) #Will Take Inp
except ValueError:
    exit("\nHy! That's Not A Number") #Error Message
else:
    print("\n") #Print New Line

#Checking Using Option
if(userInput == 1): #This Option Will Print List Of Students
    print("List Students\n")
    for students in listStd:
        print("=> {}".format(students))

elif(userInput == 2): #This Option Will Add New Student In The List
    newStd = input("Enter New Student: ")
    if(newStd in listStd): #This Condition Checking The New Student Is Alrea
        print("\nThis Student {} Already In The Database".format(newStd))   #
    else:
        listStd.append(newStd)
        print("\n=> New Student {} Successfully Add \n".format(newStd))
        for students in listStd:
            print("=> {}".format(students))

elif(userInput == 3): #This Option Will Search Student From The List
    srcStd = input("Enter Student Name To Search: ")
    if(srcStd in listStd): #This Condition Searching The Student
        print("\n=> Record Found Of Student {}".format(srcStd))
    else:
        print("\n=> No Record Found Of Student {}".format(srcStd)) #Error Me

elif(userInput == 4): #This Option Will Remove Student From The List
    rmStd = input("Enter Student Name To Remove: ")
    if(rmStd in listStd): #This Condition Removing The Student From The List
        listStd.remove(rmStd)

        print("\n=> Student {} Successfully Deleted \n".format(rmStd))
        for students in listStd:
            print("=> {}".format(students))
    else:
        print("\n=> No Record Found of This Student {}".format(rmStd)) #Er

elif(userInput < 1 or userInput > 4): #Validating User Option
    print("Please Enter Valid Option")  #Error Message
```

```
#brought to you by code-projects.org
manageStudent()

def runAgain(): #Making Runable Problem1353
    runAgn = input("\nwant To Run Again Y/n: ")
    if(runAgn.lower() == 'y'):
        if(platform.system() == "Windows"): #Checking User OS For Clearing The
            print(os.system('cls'))
        else:
            print(os.system('clear'))
        manageStudent()
        runAgain()
    else:
        quit(bye) #Print GoodBye Message And Exit The Program

runAgain()
```

Output

```
|=============================================================|
|========= Welcome To Student Management System =========|
|=============================================================|
-------------------------------------------------------------

Enter 1 : To View Student's List
Enter 2 : To Add New Student
Enter 3 : To Search Student
Enter 4 : To Remove Student

Please Select An Above Option:
```

12.5 Sales Prediction by Neural Network

Example Lemon Sales

Excel Data lemons.csv

Weekend	Sunny	Warm	BigSign	Price	NumberSold
1	0	0	1	9	71
1	1	1	0	10	137

0	1	0	0	10	0
1	0	0	1	6	107
1	0	0	1	8	80
1	1	0	0	6	110
1	1	1	0	8	167
0	0	1	1	8	0
1	0	1	0	8	124
1	1	0	0	7	95
0	0	1	1	9	0
0	0	1	0	8	0
0	0	1	1	9	0
0	0	1	1	6	0
0	1	0	1	10	0
0	1	1	1	9	0
1	0	0	1	10	65
1	0	0	1	7	92
1	0	0	0	10	50

```
import torch
from torch import nn

# Import visualization library
import matplotlib.pyplot as plt
import pandas as pd
import torch.optim as optim
```

```python
device = 'cuda' if torch.cuda.is_available() else 'cpu'
print('A {} device was detected.'.format(device))

if device=='cuda':
  print (torch.cuda.get_device_name(device=device))

# Read Data from CSV file

df = pd.read_csv("lemons.csv")
print(df)

# See first 10 rows of the dataset

p=df.head(10)
print(p)

# Cind size/shape of our dataset

q=df.shape
print(q)

# Calculate the mean and standard deviation  of price
column

priceMean = df['Price'].mean()
priceStd = df['Price'].std()
```

```python
df['Price'] = (df['Price']-priceMean)/priceStd

# Calculate the mean and standard deviation of the no of
Sold column

numSoldMean = df['NumberSold'].mean()
numSoldStd = df['NumberSold'].std()
df['NumberSold']                    =                    (df['NumberSold']-
numSoldMean)/numSoldStd

# Neural Network Training

# Extract out inputs of csv

inputs = ['Weekend','Sunny','Warm','BigSign','Price']

# make x as input with torch module

x                                                        =
torch.tensor(df[inputs].values,dtype=torch.float,device=devic
e)

# output y No of lemons sold with torch module

outputs = ['NumberSold']
```

```python
y     =     torch.tensor(df[outputs].values,dtype=torch.float,
device=device)

# Find the first 5 inputs

x[0:5]

# Find the first 5 outputs

y[0:5]

# Build  Neural Network with Inputs: 5, Outputs: 1

# Hidden Units: 100,Hidden Layers: 1, Activation Function:
Relu


model = nn.Sequential(
        nn.Linear(5,100),
        nn.ReLU(),
        nn.Linear(100,1)
    )

model.to(device)

# Train your Neural Network
```

```python
# find mean square error

criterion = torch.nn.MSELoss()

# Train with simple SGD optimizer

optimizer  =  optim.SGD(model.parameters(),  lr=0.01,
momentum=0.9)

# Train entire dataset 5 times

for epoch in range(5):
    totalLoss = 0
    for i in range(len(x)):
        ypred = model(x[i])

# Find predicted value vs the actual value & loss

        loss = criterion(ypred, y[i])

        totalLoss+=loss.item()

# Update the neural network depending on loss

        optimizer.zero_grad()
```

```python
        loss.backward()
        optimizer.step()

    # Print out our loss after each training iteration
    print ("Total Loss: ", totalLoss)


# plot predictions vs. true values to find    Network's
Performance

@torch.no_grad()

def graphPredictions(model, x, y , minValue, maxValue):
    model.eval()                          # Set the model to
inference mode

    predictions=[]                   # Track predictions
    actual=[]                        # Track the actual labels

    x.to(device)
    y.to(device)
    model.to(device)


    for i in range(len(x)):
        # Single forward pass
        pred = model(x[i])
```

```python
    # Un-normalize our prediction
    pred = pred*numSoldStd+numSoldMean
    act = y[i]*numSoldStd+numSoldMean

    # Save prediction and actual label
    predictions.append(pred.tolist())


    actual.append(act.item())

  plt.scatter(actual, predictions)
  plt.xlabel('Actual Lemonades Sold')
  plt.ylabel('Predicted Lemonades Sold')
  plt.plot([minValue,maxValue], [minValue,maxValue])
  plt.xlim(minValue, maxValue)
  plt.ylim(minValue, maxValue)

  plt.gca().set_aspect('equal', adjustable='box')
  plt.show()

  graphPredictions(model, x, y, 0, 25)

def datasetGenerator(weekend, sunny, warm, bigsign,
price):
  numlemonssold = 0
```

```python
    if weekend:
        numlemonssold = (sunny*5  + int(500 / price))
        if bigsign:
            numlemonssold = 1.3 * numlemonssold
        if warm:
            numlemonssold = 2 * numlemonssold
        if sunny:
            numlemonssold = 1.25 * numlemonssold
    numlemonssold = int(numlemonssold)


    return numlemonssold


# Data that affects the number of lemons sold in one day
weekend = 1
sunny = 0
warm = 0
bigsign = 1
price = 5


# Calculate what would have been the actual result using
# the synthetic dataset's algorithm
actual = datasetGenerator(weekend, sunny, warm, bigsign,
price)


# Use the CPU as we just need to do a single pass
model.to('cpu')
```

```python
# Normalize our inputs using the same values for our
training
price = (price - priceMean) / priceStd

# Create our input tensor
x1 = torch.tensor([weekend, sunny, warm, bigsign,
price],dtype=float)

# Pass the input into the neural network
y1 = model(x1.float())

# Un-normalize our output y1
y1 = y1*numSoldStd+numSoldMean

# Compare what your network predicted to the actual
print ("Neural Network Predicts: ", y1.item())
print ("Actual Result: ", actual)
```

Output
otal Loss: 102.22947202749782
Total Loss: 9.724280347865292
Total Loss: 5.963095147187687
Total Loss: 4.0648906094726875
Total Loss: 3.2762551852177495
Neural Network Predicts: 129.0238037109375

Actual Result: 130

12.6 Corrosion Rate Monitoring Neural Network

```python
import torch
from torch import nn

# Import visualization library
import matplotlib.pyplot as plt
import pandas as pd
import torch.optim as optim

device = 'cuda' if torch.cuda.is_available() else 'cpu'
print('A {} device was detected.'.format(device))

if device=='cuda':
  print (torch.cuda.get_device_name(device=device))

# Read Data from CSV file

df = pd.read_csv("data.csv")
#print(df)

# See first 10 rows of the dataset

p=df.head(10)
print("head=")
```

```python
print(p)

# Cind size/shape of our dataset

q=df.shape
print("shape=")
print(q)

# Calculate the mean and standard deviation   of price
column

clMean = df['Cl'].mean()
clStd = df['Cl'].std()
df['Cl'] = (df['Cl']-clMean)/clStd

# Calculate the mean and standard deviation of the no of
Sold column

icorrMean = df['Icorr'].mean()
icorrdStd = df['Icorr'].std()
df['Icorr'] = (df['Icorr']-icorrMean)/icorrdStd

# Neural Network Training

# Extract out inputs of csv
```

```python
inputs = ['Cl','SO4','O','CO3','PH']

# make x as input with torch module

x = torch.tensor(df[inputs].values,dtype=torch.float,device=device)

# output y No of lemons sold with torch module

outputs = ['Icorr']
y = torch.tensor(df[outputs].values,dtype=torch.float, device=device)

# Find the first 5 inputs

x[0:5]

# Find the first 5 outputs

y[0:5]

# Build  Neural Network with Inputs: 5, Outputs: 1

# Hidden Units: 100,Hidden Layers: 1, Activation Function: Relu
```

```
model = nn.Sequential(
        nn.Linear(5,100),
        nn.ReLU(),
        nn.Linear(100,1)
    )

model.to(device)

# Train your Neural Network

# find mean square error

criterion = torch.nn.MSELoss()

# Train  with  simple SGD optimizer

optimizer    =    optim.SGD(model.parameters(),    lr=0.01,
momentum=0.9)

# Train  entire dataset 5 times

for epoch in range(5):
    totalLoss = 0
    for i in range(len(x)):
```

```python
        ypred = model(x[i])

    # Find  predicted value  vs the actual value & loss

        loss = criterion(ypred, y[i])

        totalLoss+=loss.item()

    # Update the neural network depending on loss

        optimizer.zero_grad()
        loss.backward()
        optimizer.step()

     # Print out our loss after each training iteration
     # print ("Total Loss: ", totalLoss)

# plot  predictions  vs.  true  values  to  find    Network's
Performance

@torch.no_grad()

def graphPredictions(model, x, y , minValue, maxValue):
    model.eval()                        # Set the model to
inference mode
```

```python
predictions=[]                        # Track predictions
actual=[]                             # Track the actual labels


x.to(device)
y.to(device)
model.to(device)



for i in range(len(x)):
    # Single forward pass
    pred = model(x[i])

    # Un-normalize our prediction
    pred = pred*icorrdStd+icorrMean
    act = y[i]*icorrdStd+icorrMean

    # Save prediction and actual label
    predictions.append(pred.tolist())

    actual.append(act.item())

    print("actual=:",predictions.append(pred.tolist()))

    print("predictions=:",actual.append(act.item()))

    print(act,pred)
```

```python
plt.scatter(actual, predictions)
plt.xlabel('Actual Icorr')
plt.ylabel('Predicted Icorr')
plt.plot([minValue,maxValue], [minValue,maxValue])
plt.xlim(minValue, maxValue)
plt.ylim(minValue, maxValue)

plt.gca().set_aspect('equal', adjustable='box')
plt.show()

graphPredictions(model, x, y, 0, 300)




def datasetGenerator(cl, so4, o, co3, ph):
    icorr =30
    if cl:
        cl=cl
    if co3:
      co3 = co3
    if o:
      o=o
    if so4:
        so4 = so4
```

```python
    return icorr


# Data that affects the number of lemons sold in one day
cl = 15
so4 = 3
o = 0.14
co3 = 0.5
ph = 7


# Calculate what would have been the actual result using
# the synthetic dataset's algorithm
actual = datasetGenerator(cl, so4, o, co3, ph)


# Use the CPU as we just need to do a single pass
model.to('cpu')


# Normalize our inputs using the same values for our
training
cl = (cl - clMean) / clStd


# Create our input tensor
x1 = torch.tensor([cl, so4, o, co3, ph],dtype=float)


# Pass the input into the neural network
y1 = model(x1.float())
```

```python
# Un-normalize our output y1
y1 = (y1*icorrdStd+icorrMean)

# Compare what your network predicted to the actual
print ("Neural Network Predicts: ", y1.item())
print ("Actual Result: ", actual)
```

Output

Neural Network Predicts: 33.896

Actual Result: 30

Chapter 13

Appendix Library Modules Packages

13.1 Python Built in Functions

Python has a set of built-in functions.

Function	Description
abs()	Returns the absolute value of a number
all()	Returns True if all items in an iterable object are true
any()	Returns True if any item in an iterable object is true
ascii()	Returns a readable version of an object. Replaces none-ascii characters with escape character
bin()	Returns the binary version of a number
bool()	Returns the boolean value of the specified

	object
bytearray()	Returns an array of bytes
bytes()	Returns a bytes object
callable()	Returns True if the specified object is callable, otherwise False
chr()	Returns a character from the specified Unicode code.
classmethod()	Converts a method into a class method
compile()	Returns the specified source as an object, ready to be executed
complex()	Returns a complex number
delattr()	Deletes the specified attribute (property or method) from the specified object
dict()	Returns a dictionary (Array)
dir()	Returns a list of the specified object's properties and methods
divmod()	Returns the quotient and the remainder when argument1 is divided by argument2
enumerate()	Takes a collection (e.g. a tuple) and returns it as an enumerate object
eval()	Evaluates and executes an expression
exec()	Executes the specified code (or object)
filter()	Use a filter function to exclude items in an

	iterable object
float()	Returns a floating point number
format()	Formats a specified value
frozenset()	Returns a frozenset object
getattr()	Returns the value of the specified attribute (property or method)
globals()	Returns the current global symbol table as a dictionary
hasattr()	Returns True if the specified object has the specified attribute (property/method)
hash()	Returns the hash value of a specified object
help()	Executes the built-in help system
hex()	Converts a number into a hexadecimal value
id()	Returns the id of an object
input()	Allowing user input
int()	Returns an integer number
isinstance()	Returns True if a specified object is an instance of a specified object
issubclass()	Returns True if a specified class is a subclass of a specified object
iter()	Returns an iterator object

len()	Returns the length of an object
list()	Returns a list
locals()	Returns an updated dictionary of the current local symbol table
map()	Returns the specified iterator with the specified function applied to each item
max()	Returns the largest item in an iterable
memoryview()	Returns a memory view object
min()	Returns the smallest item in an iterable
next()	Returns the next item in an iterable
object()	Returns a new object
oct()	Converts a number into an octal
open()	Opens a file and returns a file object
ord()	Convert an integer representing the Unicode of the specified character
pow()	Returns the value of x to the power of y
print()	Prints to the standard output device
property()	Gets, sets, deletes a property
range()	Returns a sequence of numbers, starting from 0 and increments by 1 (by default)
repr()	Returns a readable version of an object
reversed()	Returns a reversed iterator
round()	Rounds a numbers

set()	Returns a new set object
setattr()	Sets an attribute (property/method) of an object
slice()	Returns a slice object
sorted()	Returns a sorted list
staticmethod()	Converts a method into a static method
str()	Returns a string object
sum()	Sums the items of an iterator
super()	Returns an object that represents the parent class
tuple()	Returns a tuple
type()	Returns the type of an object
vars()	Returns the __dict__ property of an object
zip()	Returns an iterator, from two or more iterators

13.2 Python String Function

Description

capitalize()	Converts the first character to upper case
casefold()	Converts string into lower case
center()	Returns a centered string
count()	Returns the number of times a specified

	value occurs in a string
encode()	Returns an encoded version of the string
endswith()	Returns true if the string ends with the specified value
expandtabs()	Sets the tab size of the string
find()	Searches the string for a specified value and returns the position of where it was found
format()	Formats specified values in a string
format_map()	Formats specified values in a string
index()	Searches the string for a specified value and returns the position of where it was found
isalnum()	Returns True if all characters in the string are alphanumeric
isalpha()	Returns True if all characters in the string are in the alphabet
isascii()	Returns True if all characters in the string are ascii characters
isdecimal()	Returns True if all characters in the string are decimals
isdigit()	Returns True if all characters in the string are digits

isidentifier()	Returns True if the string is an identifier
islower()	Returns True if all characters in the string are lower case
isnumeric()	Returns True if all characters in the string are numeric
isprintable()	Returns True if all characters in the string are printable
isspace()	Returns True if all characters in the string are whitespaces
istitle()	Returns True if the string follows the rules of a title
isupper()	Returns True if all characters in the string are upper case
join()	Converts the elements of an iterable into a string
ljust()	Returns a left justified version of the string
lower()	Converts a string into lower case
lstrip()	Returns a left trim version of the string
maketrans()	Returns a translation table to be used in translations
partition()	Returns a tuple where the string is parted into three parts
replace()	Returns a string where a specified value is replaced with a specified value

rfind()	Searches the string for a specified value and returns the last position of where it was found
rindex()	Searches the string for a specified value and returns the last position of where it was found
rjust()	Returns a right justified version of the string
rpartition()	Returns a tuple where the string is parted into three parts
rsplit()	Splits the string at the specified separator, and returns a list
rstrip()	Returns a right trim version of the string
split()	Splits the string at the specified separator, and returns a list
splitlines()	Splits the string at line breaks and returns a list
startswith()	Returns true if the string starts with the specified value
strip()	Returns a trimmed version of the string
swapcase()	Swaps cases, lower case becomes upper case and vice versa
title()	Converts the first character of each word to upper case

translate()	Returns a translated string
upper()	Converts a string into upper case
zfill()	Fills the string with a specified number of 0 values at the beginning

13.3 Python Dictionary Methods

Python has a set of built-in methods that you can use on dictionaries.

Method	Description
clear()	Removes all the elements from the dictionary
copy()	Returns a copy of the dictionary
fromkeys()	Returns a dictionary with the specified keys and value
get()	Returns the value of the specified key
items()	Returns a list containing a tuple for each key value pair
keys()	Returns a list containing the dictionary's keys
pop()	Removes the element with the specified key
popitem()	Removes the last inserted key-value pair
setdefault()	Returns the value of the specified key. If the key does not exist: insert the key, with the specified value

Method	Description
update()	Updates the dictionary with the specified key-value pairs
values()	Returns a list of all the values in the dictionary

13.4 Python File Methods

ython has a set of methods available for the file object.

Method	Description
close()	Closes the file
detach()	Returns the separated raw stream from the buffer
fileno()	Returns a number that represents the stream, from the operating system's perspective
flush()	Flushes the internal buffer
isatty()	Returns whether the file stream is interactive or not
read()	Returns the file content
readable()	Returns whether the file stream can be read or not
readline()	Returns one line from the file
readlines()	Returns a list of lines from the file
seek()	Change the file position
seekable()	Returns whether the file allows us to change the file position

tell()	Returns the current file position
truncate()	Resizes the file to a specified size
writable()	Returns whether the file can be written to or not
write()	Writes the specified string to the file
writelines()	Writes a list of strings to the file

13.5 Python List/Array Methods

Method	Description
append()	Adds an element at the end of the list
clear()	Removes all the elements from the list
copy()	Returns a copy of the list
count()	Returns the number of elements with the specified value
extend()	Add the elements of a list (or any iterable), to the end of the current list
index()	Returns the index of the first element with the specified value
insert()	Adds an element at the specified position
pop()	Removes the element at the specified position
remove()	Removes the first item with the specified value
reverse()	Reverses the order of the list
sort()	Sorts the list

13.6 Python math Module

Python has a built-in module that you can use for mathematical tasks.

The math module has a set of methods and constants.

Math Methods

Method	Description
math.acos()	Returns the arc cosine of a number
math.acosh()	Returns the inverse hyperbolic cosine of a number
math.asin()	Returns the arc sine of a number
math.asinh()	Returns the inverse hyperbolic sine of a number
math.atan()	Returns the arc tangent of a number in radians
math.atan2()	Returns the arc tangent of y/x in radians
math.atanh()	Returns the inverse hyperbolic tangent of a number
math.ceil()	Rounds a number up to the nearest integer
math.comb()	Returns the number of ways to choose

	k items from n items without repetition and order
math.copysign()	Returns a float consisting of the value of the first parameter and the sign of the second parameter
math.cos()	Returns the cosine of a number
math.cosh()	Returns the hyperbolic cosine of a number
math.degrees()	Converts an angle from radians to degrees
math.dist()	Returns the Euclidean distance between two points (p and q), where p and q are the coordinates of that point
math.erf()	Returns the error function of a number
math.erfc()	Returns the complementary error function of a number
math.exp()	Returns E raised to the power of x
math.expm1()	Returns E^x - 1
math.fabs()	Returns the absolute value of a number
math.factorial()	Returns the factorial of a number
math.floor()	Rounds a number down to the nearest integer
math.fmod()	Returns the remainder of x/y

math.frexp()	Returns the mantissa and the exponent, of a specified number
math.fsum()	Returns the sum of all items in any iterable (tuples, arrays, lists, etc.)
math.gamma()	Returns the gamma function at x
math.gcd()	Returns the greatest common divisor of two integers
math.hypot()	Returns the Euclidean norm
math.isclose()	Checks whether two values are close to each other, or not
math.isfinite()	Checks whether a number is finite or not
math.isinf()	Checks whether a number is infinite or not
math.isnan()	Checks whether a value is NaN (not a number) or not
math.isqrt()	Rounds a square root number downwards to the nearest integer
math.ldexp()	Returns the inverse of math.frexp() which is x * (2**i) of the given numbers x and i
math.lgamma()	Returns the log gamma value of x
math.log()	Returns the natural logarithm of a

	number, or the logarithm of number to base
math.log10()	Returns the base-10 logarithm of x
math.log1p()	Returns the natural logarithm of 1+x
math.log2()	Returns the base-2 logarithm of x
math.perm()	Returns the number of ways to choose k items from n items with order and without repetition
math.pow()	Returns the value of x to the power of y
math.prod()	Returns the product of all the elements in an iterable
math.radians()	Converts a degree value into radians
math.remainder()	Returns the closest value that can make numerator completely divisible by the denominator
math.sin()	Returns the sine of a number
math.sinh()	Returns the hyperbolic sine of a number
math.sqrt()	Returns the square root of a number
math.tan()	Returns the tangent of a number
math.tanh()	Returns the hyperbolic tangent of a number
math.trunc()	Returns the truncated integer parts of a

number

Math Constants

Constant	Description
math.e	Returns Euler's number (2.7182...)
math.inf	Returns a floating-point positive infinity
math.nan	Returns a floating-point NaN (Not a Number) value
math.pi	Returns PI (3.1415...)
math.tau	Returns tau (6.2831...)

Modules

13.7 NumPy

The NumPy library is the core library for scientific computing in

Python. It provides a high-performance multidimensional array

1D array

2D array

3D array

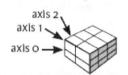

Creating Arrays

```
>>> a = np.array([1,2,3])
>>> b = np.array([(1.5,2,3), (4,5,6)], dtype = float)
>>> c = np.array([[(1.5,2,3), (4,5,6)], [(3,2,1), (4,5,6)]],
            dtype = float)
```

Initial Placeholders

`>>> np.zeros((3,4))`	Create an array of zeros
`>>> np.ones((2,3,4),dtype=np.int16)`	Create an array of ones
`>>> d = np.arange(10,25,5)`	Create an array of evenly spaced values (step value)
`>>> np.linspace(0,2,9)`	Create an array of evenly spaced values (number of samples)
`>>> e = np.full((2,2),7)`	Create a constant array
`>>> f = np.eye(2)`	Create a 2X2 identity matrix
`>>> np.random.random((2,2))`	Create an array with random values
`>>> np.empty((3,2))`	Create an empty array

Saving & Loading On Disk

```
>>> np.save('my_array', a)
>>> np.savez('array.npz', a, b)
>>> np.load('my_array.npy')
```

Saving & Loading Text Files

```
>>> np.loadtxt("myfile.txt")
>>> np.genfromtxt("my_file.csv", delimiter=',')
>>> np.savetxt("myarray.txt", a, delimiter=" ")
```

Data Types

`>>> np.int64`	Signed 64-bit integer types
`>>> np.float32`	Standard double-precision floating point
`>>> np.complex`	Complex numbers represented by 128 floats
`>>> np.bool`	Boolean type storing TRUE and FALSE values
`>>> np.object`	Python object type
`>>> np.string_`	Fixed-length string type
`>>> np.unicode_`	Fixed-length unicode type

`>>> a.shape`	Array dimensions
`>>> len(a)`	Length of array
`>>> b.ndim`	Number of array dimensions
`>>> e.size`	Number of array elements
`>>> b.dtype`	Data type of array elements
`>>> b.dtype.name`	Name of data type
`>>> b.astype(int)`	Convert an array to a different type

Arithmetic Operations

`>>> g = a - b`
`array([[-0.5, 0. , 0. ],`
`       [-3. , -3. , -3. ]])`
	Subtraction

`>>> np.subtract(a,b)`	Subtraction

`>>> b + a`
`array([[ 2.5, 4. , 6. ],`
`       [ 5. , 7. , 9. ]])`
	Addition

`>>> np.add(b,a)`	Addition

`>>> a / b`
`array([[ 0.66666667, 1.      , 1.      ],`
`       [ 0.25      , 0.4     , 0.5     ]])`
	Division

`>>> np.divide(a,b)`	Division

`>>> a * b`
`array([[ 1.5, 4. , 9. ],`
`       [ 4. , 10. , 18. ]])`
	Multiplication

`>>> np.multiply(a,b)`	Multiplication
`>>> np.exp(b)`	Exponentiation
`>>> np.sqrt(b)`	Square root
`>>> np.sin(a)`	Print sines of an array
`>>> np.cos(b)`	Element-wise cosine
`>>> np.log(a)`	Element-wise natural logarithm

`>>> e.dot(f)`
`array([[ 7., 7.],`
`       [ 7., 7.]])`
	Dot product

Aggregate Functions

`>>> a.sum()`	Array-wise sum
`>>> a.min()`	Array-wise minimum value
`>>> b.max(axis=0)`	Maximum value of an array row
`>>> b.cumsum(axis=1)`	Cumulative sum of the elements
`>>> a.mean()`	Mean
`>>> b.median()`	Median
`>>> a.corrcoef()`	Correlation coefficient
`>>> np.std(b)`	Standard deviation

Aggregate Functions

`>>> a.sum()`	Array-wise sum
`>>> a.min()`	Array-wise minimum value
`>>> b.max(axis=0)`	Maximum value of an array row
`>>> b.cumsum(axis=1)`	Cumulative sum of the elements
`>>> a.mean()`	Mean
`>>> b.median()`	Median
`>>> a.corrcoef()`	Correlation coefficient
`>>> np.std(b)`	Standard deviation

Copying Arrays

`>>> h = a.view()`	Create a view of the array with the same data
`>>> np.copy(a)`	Create a copy of the array
`>>> h = a.copy()`	Create a deep copy of the array

Sorting Arrays

`>>> a.sort()`	Sort an array
`>>> c.sort(axis=0)`	Sort the elements of an array's axis

Subsetting, Slicing, Indexing

Subsetting

```
>>> a[2]
 3
```
Select the element at the 2nd index

```
>>> b[1,2]
 6.0
```
Select the element at row 1 column 2
(equivalent to `b[1][2]`)

Slicing

```
>>> a[0:2]
 array([1, 2])
```
Select items at index 0 and 1

```
>>> b[0:2,1]
 array([ 2.,   5.])
```
Select items at rows 0 and 1 in column 1

```
>>> b[:1]
 array([[1.5, 2., 3.]])
```
Select all items at row 0
(equivalent to `b[0:1, :]`)

```
>>> c[1,...]
 array([[[ 3.,   2.,   1.],
         [ 4.,   5.,   6.]]])
```
Same as `[1,:,:]`

```
>>> a[ : :-1]
 array([3, 2, 1])
```
Reversed array `a`

Boolean Indexing

```
>>> a[a<2]
 array([1])
```
Select elements from `a` less than 2

Fancy Indexing

```
>>> b[[1, 0, 1, 0],[0, 1, 2, 0]]
 array([ 4. , 2. , 6. , 1.5])
```
Select elements (1,0),(0,1),(1,2) and (0,0)

```
>>> b[[1, 0, 1, 0]][:,[0,1,2,0]]
 array([[ 4. , 5. , 6. , 4. ],
        [ 1.5, 2. , 3. , 1.5],
        [ 4. , 5. , 6. , 4. ],
        [ 1.5, 2. , 3. , 1.5]])
```
Select a subset of the matrix's rows
and columns

Array Manipulation

Transposing Array

```
>>> i = np.transpose(b)
>>> i.T
```
Permute array dimensions
Permute array dimensions

Changing Array Shape

```
>>> b.ravel()
>>> g.reshape(3,-2)
```
Flatten the array
Reshape, but don't change data

Adding/Removing Elements

```
>>> h.resize((2,6))
>>> np.append(h,g)
>>> np.insert(a, 1, 5)
>>> np.delete(a,[1])
```
Return a new array with shape (2,6)
Append items to an array
Insert items in an array
Delete items from an array

Combining Arrays

```
>>> np.concatenate((a,d),axis=0)
 array([ 1,  2,  3, 10, 15, 20])
```
Concatenate arrays

```
>>> np.vstack((a,b))
 array([[ 1. ,  2. ,  3. ],
        [ 1.5,  2. ,  3. ],
        [ 4. ,  5. ,  6. ]])
```
Stack arrays vertically (row-wise)

```
>>> np.r_[e,f]
>>> np.hstack((e,f))
 array([[ 7.,  7.,  1.,  0.],
        [ 7.,  7.,  0.,  1.]])
```
Stack arrays vertically (row-wise)
Stack arrays horizontally (column-wise)

```
>>> np.column_stack((a,d))
 array([[ 1, 10],
        [ 2, 15],
        [ 3, 20]])
```
Create stacked column-wise arrays

```
>>> np.c_[a,d]
```
Create stacked column-wise arrays

Splitting Arrays

```
>>> np.hsplit(a,3)
 [array([1]),array([2]),array([3])]
```
Split the array horizontally at the 3rd index

```
>>> np.vsplit(c,2)
[array([[[ 1.5,  2. ,  1. ],
         [ 4. ,  5. ,  6. ]]]),
  array([[[ 3.,  2.,  3.],
          [ 4.,  5.,  6.]]])]
```
Split the array vertically at the 2nd index

13.8 Pandas Data Frame

Creating DataFrames

	a	b	c
1	4	7	10
2	5	8	11
3	6	9	12

```
df = pd.DataFrame(
        {"a" : [4, 5, 6],
         "b" : [7, 8, 9],
         "c" : [10, 11, 12]},
        index = [1, 2, 3])
```
Specify values for each column.

```
df = pd.DataFrame(
     [[4, 7, 10],
      [5, 8, 11],
      [6, 9, 12]],
     index=[1, 2, 3],
     columns=['a', 'b', 'c'])
```
Specify values for each row.

n	v	a	b	c
d	1	4	7	10
	2	5	8	11
e	2	6	9	12

```
df = pd.DataFrame(
        {"a" : [4 ,5, 6],
         "b" : [7, 8, 9],
         "c" : [10, 11, 12]},
index = pd.MultiIndex.from_tuples(
        [('d', 1), ('d', 2),
         ('e', 2)], names=['n', 'v']))
```
Create DataFrame with a MultiIndex

Reshaping Data – Change layout, sorting, reindexing, renaming

pd.melt(df)
Gather columns into rows.

df.pivot(columns='var', values='val')
Spread rows into columns.

df.sort_values('mpg')
Order rows by values of a column (low to high).

df.sort_values('mpg', ascending=False)
Order rows by values of a column (high to low).

df.rename(columns = {'y':'year'})
Rename the columns of a DataFrame

df.sort_index()
Sort the index of a DataFrame

df.reset_index()
Reset index of DataFrame to row numbers, moving index to columns.

pd.concat([df1,df2])
Append rows of DataFrames

pd.concat([df1,df2], axis=1)
Append columns of DataFrames

df.drop(columns=['Length', 'Height'])
Drop columns from DataFrame

Subset Observations - rows

df[df.Length > 7]
Extract rows that meet logical criteria.
df.drop_duplicates()
Remove duplicate rows (only considers columns).
df.sample(frac=0.5)
Randomly select fraction of rows.
df.sample(n=10) Randomly select n rows.
df.nlargest(n, 'value')
Select and order top n entries.
df.nsmallest(n, 'value')
Select and order bottom n entries.
df.head(n)
Select first n rows.
df.tail(n)
Select last n rows.

Subset Variables - columns

df[['width', 'length', 'species']]
Select multiple columns with specific names.
df['width'] or df.width
Select single column with specific name.
df.filter(regex='regex')
Select columns whose name matches
regular expression regex.

Using query

query() allows Boolean expressions for filtering
rows.
df.query('Length > 7')
df.query('Length > 7 and Width < 8')
df.query('Name.str.startswith("abc")',
engine="python")

Subsets - rows and columns

Use df.loc[] and df.iloc[] to select only
rows, only columns or both.
Use df.at[] and df.iat[] to access a single
value by row and column.
First index selects rows, second index columns.

df.iloc[10:20]
Select rows 10-20.
df.iloc[:, [1, 2, 5]]
Select columns in positions 1, 2 and 5 (first
column is 0).
df.loc[:, 'x2':'x4']
Select all columns between x2 and x4 (inclusive)
df.loc[df['a'] > 10, ['a', 'c']]
Select rows meeting logical condition, and only
the specific columns .
df.iat[1, 2] Access single value by index
df.at[4, 'A'] Access single value by label

Logic in Python (and pandas)				regex (Regular Expressions) Examples
<	Less than	!=	Not equal to	'\.'	Matches strings containing a period '.'
>	Greater than	df.column.isin(values)	Group membership	'Length$'	Matches strings ending with word 'Length'
==	Equals	pd.isnull(obj)	Is NaN	'^Sepal'	Matches strings beginning with the word 'Sepal'
<=	Less than or equals	pd.notnull(obj)	Is not NaN	'^x[1-5]$'	Matches strings beginning with 'x' and ending with 1,2,3,4,5
>=	Greater than or equals	&,|,~,^,df.any(),df.all()	Logical and, or, not, xor, any, all	'^(?!Species$).*'	Matches strings except the string 'Species'

Summarize Data

`df['w'].value counts()`
Count number of rows with each unique value of variable

`len(df)`
# of rows in DataFrame.

`df.shape`
Tuple of # of rows, # of columns in DataFrame.

`df['w'].nunique()`
# of distinct values in a column.

`df.describe()`
Basic descriptive and statistics for each column (or GroupBy).

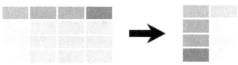

pandas provides a large set of summary functions that operate on different kinds of pandas objects (DataFrame columns, Series, GroupBy, Expanding and Rolling (see below)) and produce single values for each of the groups. When applied to a DataFrame, the result is returned as a pandas Series for each column. Examples:

`sum()`
Sum values of each object.

`count()`
Count non-NA/null values of each object.

`median()`
Median value of each object.

`quantile([0.25,0.75])`
Quantiles of each object.

`apply(function)`
Apply function to each object.

`min()`
Minimum value in each object.

`max()`
Maximum value in each object.

`mean()`
Mean value of each object.

`var()`
Variance of each object.

`std()`
Standard deviation of each object.

Handling Missing Data

`df.dropna()`

    Drop rows with any column having NA/null data.

`df.fillna(value)`

    Replace all NA/null data with value.

Make New Columns

`df.assign(Area=lambda df: df.Length*df.Height)`

    Compute and append one or more new columns.

`df['Volume'] = df.Length*df.Height*df.Depth`

    Add single column.

`pd.qcut(df.col, n, labels=False)`

    Bin column into n buckets.

pandas provides a large set of **vector functions** that operate on all columns of a DataFrame or a single selected column (a pandas Series). These functions produce vectors of values for each of the columns, or a single Series for the individual Series. Examples:

`max(axis=1)`

    Element-wise max.

`min(axis=1)`

    Element-wise min.

`clip(lower=-10,upper=10)` `abs()`

    Trim values at input thresholds   Absolute value.

Combine Data Sets

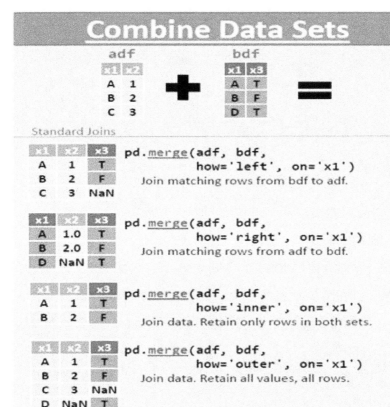

adf
x1	x2
A	1
B	2
C	3

bdf
x1	x3
A	T
B	F
D	T

Standard Joins

x1	x2	x3
A	1	T
B	2	F
C	3	NaN

```
pd.merge(adf, bdf,
         how='left', on='x1')
```
Join matching rows from bdf to adf.

x1	x2	x3
A	1.0	T
B	2.0	F
D	NaN	T

```
pd.merge(adf, bdf,
         how='right', on='x1')
```
Join matching rows from adf to bdf.

x1	x2	x3
A	1	T
B	2	F

```
pd.merge(adf, bdf,
         how='inner', on='x1')
```
Join data. Retain only rows in both sets.

x1	x2	x3
A	1	T
B	2	F
C	3	NaN
D	NaN	T

```
pd.merge(adf, bdf,
         how='outer', on='x1')
```
Join data. Retain all values, all rows.

Filtering Joins

x1	x2
A	1
B	2

```
adf[adf.x1.isin(bdf.x1)]
```
All rows in adf that have a match in bdf.

x1	x2
C	3

```
adf[~adf.x1.isin(bdf.x1)]
```
All rows in adf that do not have a match in bdf.

ydf
x1	x2
A	1
B	2
C	3

zdf
x1	x2
B	2
C	3
D	4

Set-like Operations

x1	x2
B	2
C	3

```
pd.merge(ydf, zdf)
```
Rows that appear in both ydf and zdf
(Intersection).

x1	x2
A	1
B	2
C	3
D	4

```
pd.merge(ydf, zdf, how='outer')
```
Rows that appear in either or both ydf and zdf
(Union).

x1	x2
A	1

```
pd.merge(ydf, zdf, how='outer',
         indicator=True)
.query('_merge == "left_only"')
.drop(columns=['_merge'])
```
Rows that appear in ydf but not zdf (Setdiff).

Group Data

df.groupby(by="col") Return a GroupBy object, grouped by values in column named "col".	The examples below can also be applied to groups. In this case, the function is applied on a per-group basis, and the returned vectors are of the length of the original DataFrame.

df.groupby(level="ind") Return a GroupBy object, grouped by values in index level named "ind".	**shift(1)** Copy with values shifted by 1. **rank(method='dense')** Ranks with no gaps. **rank(method='min')** Ranks. Ties get min rank. **rank(pct=True)** Ranks rescaled to interval [0, 1]. **rank(method='first')** Ranks. Ties go to first value.	**shift(-1)** Copy with values lagged by 1. **cumsum()** Cumulative sum. **cummax()** Cumulative max. **cummin()** Cumulative min. **cumprod()** Cumulative product.
size() Size of each group. o a group.		
agg(function**)** Aggregate group using function.		

13.9 Matplotlib

It is a Python 2D plotting library which produces publication-quality figures in a variety of hardcopy formats

Colors, Color Bars & Color Maps

```
>>> plt.plot(x, x, x, x**2, x, x**3)
>>> ax.plot(x, y, alpha = 0.4)
>>> ax.plot(x, y, c='k')
>>> fig.colorbar(im, orientation='horizontal')
>>> im = ax.imshow(img,
                   cmap='seismic')
```

Markers

```
>>> fig, ax = plt.subplots()
>>> ax.scatter(x,y,marker=".")
>>> ax.plot(x,y,marker="o")
```

Linestyles

```
>>> plt.plot(x,y,linewidth=4.0)
>>> plt.plot(x,y,ls='solid')
>>> plt.plot(x,y,ls='--')
>>> plt.plot(x,y,'--',x**2,y**2,'-.')
>>> plt.setp(lines,color='r',linewidth=4.0)
```

Text & Annotations

```
>>> ax.text(1,
            -2.1,
            'Example Graph',
            style='italic')
>>> ax.annotate("Sine",
                xy=(8, 0),
                xycoords='data',
                xytext=(10.5, 0),
                textcoords='data',
                arrowprops=dict(arrowstyle="->",
                                connectionstyle="arc3"),)
```

Save Plot

Save figures
```
>> plt.savefig('foo.png')
```
Save transparent figures
```
>> plt.savefig('foo.png', transparent=    )
```

Show Plot
```
·>> plt.show()
```

13.10 Scikit-learn

Scikit-learn is an open source Python library that implements a range of machine learning

A Basic Example

```
>>> from sklearn import neighbors, datasets, preprocessing
>>> from sklearn.model_selection import train_test_split
>>> from sklearn.metrics import accuracy_score
>>> iris = datasets.load_iris()
>>> X, y = iris.data[:, :2], iris.target
>>> X_train, X_test, y_train, y_test = train_test_split(X, y, random_state=33)
>>> scaler = preprocessing.StandardScaler().fit(X_train)
>>> X_train = scaler.transform(X_train)
>>> X_test = scaler.transform(X_test)
>>> knn = neighbors.KNeighborsClassifier(n_neighbors=5)
>>> knn.fit(X_train, y_train)
>>> y_pred = knn.predict(X_test)
>>> accuracy_score(y_test, y_pred)
```

Training And Test Data

```
>>> import numpy as np
>>> X = np.random.random((10,5))
>>> y = np.array(['M','M','F','F','M','F','M','M','F','F','F'])
>>> X[X < 0.7] = 0
>>> from sklearn.model_selection import train_test_split
>>> X_train, X_test, y_train, y_test = train_test_split(X, y, random_state=0)
```

Model Fitting

Supervised learning	
`>>> lr.fit(X, y)`	Fit the model to the data
`>>> knn.fit(X_train, y_train)`	
`>>> svc.fit(X_train, y_train)`	
Unsupervised Learning	
`>>> k_means.fit(X_train)`	Fit the model to the data
`>>> pca_model = pca.fit_transform(X_train)`	Fit to data, then transform it

Prediction

Supervised Estimators	
`>>> y_pred = svc.predict(np.random.random((2,5)))`	Predict labels
`>>> y_pred = lr.predict(X_test)`	Predict labels
`>>> y_pred = knn.predict_proba(X_test)`	Estimate probability of a label
Unsupervised Estimators	
`>>> y_pred = k_means.predict(X_test)`	Predict labels in clustering algos

Preprocessing The Data

Standardization

```
>>> from sklearn.preprocessing import StandardScaler
>>> scaler = StandardScaler().fit(X_train)
>>> standardized_X = scaler.transform(X_train)
>>> standardized_X_test = scaler.transform(X_test)
```

Encoding Categorical Features

```
>>> from sklearn.preprocessing import LabelEncoder
>>> enc = LabelEncoder()
>>> y = enc.fit_transform(y)
```

Normalization

```
>>> from sklearn.preprocessing import Normalizer
>>> scaler = Normalizer().fit(X_train)
>>> normalized_X = scaler.transform(X_train)
>>> normalized_X_test = scaler.transform(X_test)
```

Imputing Missing Values

```
>>> from sklearn.preprocessing import Imputer
>>> imp = Imputer(missing_values=0, strategy='mean', axis=0)
>>> imp.fit_transform(X_train)
```

Binarization

```
>>> from sklearn.preprocessing import Binarizer
>>> binarizer = Binarizer(threshold=0.0).fit(X)
>>> binary_X = binarizer.transform(X)
```

Generating Polynomial Features

```
>>> from sklearn.preprocessing import PolynomialFeatures
>>> poly = PolynomialFeatures(5)
>>> poly.fit_transform(X)
```

Evaluate Your Model's Performance

Classification Metrics

Accuracy Score

`>>> knn.score(X_test, y_test)`	Estimator score method
`>>> from sklearn.metrics import accuracy_score` `>>> accuracy_score(y_test, y_pred)`	Metric scoring functions
Classification Report	
`>>> from sklearn.metrics import classification_report` `>>> print(classification_report(y_test, y_pred))`	Precision, recall, f1-score and support

Confusion Matrix

```
>>> from sklearn.metrics import confusion_matrix
>>> print(confusion_matrix(y_test, y_pred))
```

Regression Metrics

Mean Absolute Error

```
>>> from sklearn.metrics import mean_absolute_error
>>> y_true = [3, -0.5, 2]
>>> mean_absolute_error(y_true, y_pred)
```

Mean Squared Error

```
>>> from sklearn.metrics import mean_squared_error
>>> mean_squared_error(y_test, y_pred)
```

R^2 Score

```
>>> from sklearn.metrics import r2_score
>>> r2_score(y_true, y_pred)
```

Clustering Metrics

Adjusted Rand Index

```
>>> from sklearn.metrics import adjusted_rand_score
>>> adjusted_rand_score(y_true, y_pred)
```

Homogeneity

```
>>> from sklearn.metrics import homogeneity_score
>>> homogeneity_score(y_true, y_pred)
```

V-measure

```
>>> from sklearn.metrics import v_measure_score
>>> metrics.v_measure_score(y_true, y_pred)
```

Cross-Validation

```
>>> from sklearn.cross_validation import cross_val_score
>>> print(cross_val_score(knn, X_train, y_train, cv=4))
>>> print(cross_val_score(lr, X, y, cv=2))
```

Tune Your Model

Grid Search

```
>>> from sklearn.grid_search import GridSearchCV
>>> params = {"n_neighbors": np.arange(1,3),
              "metric": ["euclidean", "cityblock"]}
>>> grid = GridSearchCV(estimator=knn,
                        param_grid=params)
>>> grid.fit(X_train, y_train)
>>> print(grid.best_score_)
>>> print(grid.best_estimator_.n_neighbors)
```

Randomized Parameter Optimization

```
>>> from sklearn.grid_search import RandomizedSearchCV
>>> params = {"n_neighbors": range(1,5),
              "weights": ["uniform", "distance"]}
>>> rsearch = RandomizedSearchCV(estimator=knn,
                                 param_distributions=params,
                                 cv=4,
                                 n_iter=8,
                                 random_state=5)
>>> rsearch.fit(X_train, y_train)
>>> print(rsearch.best_score_)
```

13.11 Keras Cheat Sheet

Keras is a powerful and easy-to-use deep learning library forTheano and TensorFlow that provides a high-level neural networks

A Basic Example

```
>>> import numpy as np
>>> from tensorflow.keras.models import Sequential
>>> from tensorflow.keras.layers import Dense
>>> data = np.random.random((1000,100))
>>> labels = np.random.randint(2,size=(1000,1))
>>> model = Sequential()
>>> model.add(Dense(32,
                    activation='relu',
                    input_dim=100))
>>> model.add(Dense(1, activation='sigmoid'))
>>> model.compile(optimizer='rmsprop',
                  loss='binary_crossentropy',
                  metrics=['accuracy'])
>>> model.fit(data,labels,epochs=10,batch_size=32)
>>> predictions = model.predict(data)
```

Sequence Padding

```
>>> from tensorflow.keras.preprocessing import sequence
>>> x_train4 = sequence.pad_sequences(x_train4,maxlen=80)
>>> x_test4 = sequence.pad_sequences(x_test4,maxlen=80)
```

One-Hot Encoding

```
>>> from tensorflow.keras.utils import to_categorical
>>> Y_train = to_categorical(y_train, num_classes)
>>> Y_test = to_categorical(y_test, num_classes)
>>> Y_train3 = to_categorical(y_train3, num_classes)
>>> Y_test3 = to_categorical(y_test3, num_classes)
```

> Model Architecture

Sequential Model

```
>>> from tensorflow.keras.models import Sequential
>>> model = Sequential()
>>> model2 = Sequential()
>>> model3 = Sequential()
```

Multilayer Perceptron (MLP)

Binary Classification

```
>>> from tensorflow.keras.layers import Dense
>>> model.add(Dense(12,
                    input_dim=8,
                    kernel_initializer='uniform',
                    activation='relu'))
>>> model.add(Dense(8,kernel_initializer='uniform',activation='relu'))
>>> model.add(Dense(1,kernel_initializer='uniform',activation='sigmoid')
```

Multi-Class Classification

```
>>> from tensorflow.keras.layers import Dropout
>>> model.add(Dense(512,activation='relu',input_shape=(784,)))
>>> model.add(Dropout(0.2))
>>> model.add(Dense(512,activation='relu'))
>>> model.add(Dropout(0.2))
>>> model.add(Dense(10,activation='softmax'))
```

Regression

```
>>> model.add(Dense(64,activation='relu',input_dim=train_data.shape[1]))
>>> model.add(Dense(1))
```

13.12 Neural Network for Image Processing

Convolutional Neural Network (CNN)

```
>>> from tensorflow.keras.layers import Activation,Conv2D,MaxPooling2D,Flatten
>>> model2.add(Conv2D(32,(3,3),padding='same',input_shape=x_train.shape[1:]))
>>> model2.add(Activation('relu'))
>>> model2.add(Conv2D(32,(3,3)))
>>> model2.add(Activation('relu'))
>>> model2.add(MaxPooling2D(pool_size=(2,2)))
>>> model2.add(Dropout(0.25))
>>> model2.add(Conv2D(64,(3,3), padding='same'))
>>> model2.add(Activation('relu'))
>>> model2.add(Conv2D(64,(3, 3)))
>>> model2.add(Activation('relu'))
>>> model2.add(MaxPooling2D(pool_size=(2,2)))
>>> model2.add(Dropout(0.25))
>>> model2.add(Flatten())
>>> model2.add(Dense(512))
>>> model2.add(Activation('relu'))
>>> model2.add(Dropout(0.5))
>>> model2.add(Dense(num_classes))
>>> model2.add(Activation('softmax'))
```

> Prediction

```
>>> model3.predict(x_test4, batch_size=32)
>>> model3.predict_classes(x_test4,batch_size=32)
```

> Model Training

```
>>> model3.fit(x_train4,
               y_train4,
               batch_size=32,
               epochs=15,
               verbose=1,
               validation_data=(x_test4,y_test4))
```

> Evaluate Your Model's Performance

```
>>> score = model3.evaluate(x_test,
                            y_test,
                            batch_size=32)
```

> Save/ Reload Models

```
>>> from tensorflow.keras.models import load_model
>>> model3.save('model_file.h5')
>>> my_model = load_model('my_model.h5')
```

> Model Fine-tuning

Optimization Parameters

```
>>> from tensorflow.keras.optimizers import RMSprop
>>> opt = RMSprop(lr=0.0001, decay=1e-6)
>>> model2.compile(loss='categorical_crossentropy',
                   optimizer=opt,
                   metrics=['accuracy'])
```

Early Stopping

```
>>> from tensorflow.keras.callbacks import EarlyStopping
>>> early_stopping_monitor = EarlyStopping(patience=2)
>>> model3.fit(x_train4,
               y_train4,
               batch_size=32,
               epochs=15,
               validation_data=(x_test4,y_test4),
               callbacks=[early_stopping_monitor])
```

13.3 References

1. Python for Science and Engineering CHans-Petter Halvorsen

August 12, 2020 ISBN:978-82-691106-5-4

2. Subir Paul , Electrochemical Energy Synthesis and Storage in Battery and Fuel Cell, Amazon Books,

, 2017, ☐   ISBN-10: 1520321929 ☐   ISBN-13: 978-1520321929 216 pages

3. Subir Paul , Beginner Guide to Develop Programs in C/C++ for Modeling and Simulation to Engineering Problems, Amazon Books, ISBN-13: 978-1520103884 , 2016, 445 pages

Chapter 14

Python Code Beginner Practice

14.1 Simulation

```
import numpy as np
import matplotlib.pyplot as plt


a=0.25
b=2


Ts=0.001
Tstop=1
uk=1
xk=0


N= int(Tstop/Ts)
data=[]
data.append(xk)


plt.axis([0,N,0,10])

for k in range(N):
    xk1 = (1- a*Ts )*xk + Ts*b*uk
    xk=xk1
```

```python
    data.append(xk1)
    plt.scatter (k,xk1)
    plt.pause(Ts)

plt.show ()
```

14.2 Read data from array

```python
import numpy as np
import csv

CSVData = open("data1.csv")
Array2d_result = np.loadtxt(CSVData, delimiter=",")
print(Array2d_result)

csv_filename = 'data1.csv'
with open(csv_filename) as f:
    reader = csv.reader(f)
    p= list(reader)
    print(p)
```

```python
csv_filename = 'data_o.csv'
with open(csv_filename) as f:
    reader = csv.reader(f)
    t= list(reader)
    print(t)
```

14.3 Optimization

```python
import numpy as np

import matplotlib.pyplot as plt

from scipy import optimize

xmin=-5
xmax=5
dx=0.1

N= int ((xmax-xmin)/dx)

x=np.linspace (xmin,xmax,N+1)

y=x**2 + 2*x + 1;
```

```python
plt.plot(x,y)

plt.xlim(xmin,xmax)

xxmin=-5
xxmax=5

def yy(xx):

    return xx**2 + 2*xx +1

xx_min=optimize.fminbound (yy,xxmin,xxmax)

print(xx_min)

# Result -1.0
```

14.4 Plot X vs Y

```python
import numpy as np

import matplotlib.pyplot as plt

xmin=-5
xmax=5
dx=0.1
```

```python
N= int ((xmax-xmin)/dx)

x=np.linspace (xmin,xmax,N+1)

y=x**2 + 2*x + 1;

x1=[-4,1,2,3,4,5]

y1=[30,15,10,9,6,2]

plt.plot(x,y, 'o')

plt.plot(x1,y1,'r')

plt.show()
```

14.5 Python Maths

```python
 import math
# math.log(value,base)
a = 8
b = 4
def add(a,b): # Use Editplus editor
  sum=a+b
  print(sum)
```

```python
def multiply(a,b):
    product=a*b
    print(product)

def splog(a,b):
    value=math.log(a,b)


a=10
b=20
```

14.6 Make function

```python
# function

def stat (x):
    sum=0
    for x in data :

        sum=sum + x

        N=len(data)
        mean= sum/N

        return sum , mean
```

```
data=(1,2,3,4,5)

sum, mean =stat (data)


print ( sum, mean)

# Results 15   3.0


print(add(a,b))
```